White Urban Teachers

Stories of Fear, Violence, and Desire

Audrey Lensmire

ROWMAN & LITTLEFIELD EDUCATION
A division of
ROWMAN & LITTLEFIELD PUBLISHERS, INC.
Lanham • New York • Toronto • Plymouth, UK

Published by Rowman & Littlefield Education
A division of Rowman & Littlefield Publishers, Inc.
A wholly owned subsidiary of The Rowman & Littlefield Publishing Group, Inc.
4501 Forbes Boulevard, Suite 200, Lanham, Maryland 20706
www.rowman.com

10 Thornbury Road, Plymouth PL6 7PP, United Kingdom

British Library Cataloguing in Publication Information Available

Library of Congress Cataloging-in-Publication Data

Lensmire, Audrey.
White urban teachers : stories of fear, violence, and desire / Audrey Lensmire.
p. cm.
Includes bibliographical references.
ISBN 978-1-61048-765-8 (cloth : alk. paper) -- ISBN 978-1-61048-766-5 (pbk. : alk. paper) -- ISBN
978-1-61048-767-2 (electronic)
1. Education, Urban--United States. 2. Teachers, White--United States. I. Title.
LC5131.L395 2012
370.9173'2--dc23
2012001219

The paper used in this publication meets the minimum requirements of American
National Standard for Information Sciences Permanence of Paper for Printed Library
Materials, ANSI/NISO Z39.48-1992.

Printed in the United States of America

For my daughters, Noa and Aliya Appelsies
and for my parents, Bruce and Bitsy Fell Winograd
and Charles Manaster II

The challenge for whiteness studies is how to advocate the idea of whiteness as a useful classification for examining white power and prestige without ignoring its limitations in defining and describing its subjects.
—Maurice Berger, *White Lies*

I think if I had to put a finger on what I consider a good education, a good radical education, it wouldn't be anything about methods or techniques it would be about loving people first.
—Myles Horton, *We Make the Road by Walking*

I came to theory because I was hurting.
—bell hooks, *Teaching to Transgress*

Contents

Foreword

The paradox of the white teacher who stands in front of a class of children of color haunts our educational system. In response, educators have called for reforms to increase the number of teachers of color, for better multicultural teacher education, and for the end of resegregation. While these reform efforts matter, the intransigent nature of public schooling in the United States remains: its history and current context tell us more about its usefulness as a sorting mechanism for our young people than a path to "meritocracy." Given these rules of play, certain durable stories emerge about white teachers in communities of color.

One theme is that of the white missionary teacher out to save children of color from themselves and their communities. Exemplified by notions of caring for other people's children, a kind of superiority and paternalism, I hear this theme often in the narratives of my preservice teachers. For some teachers, colorblindness is a noble theme, politically neutral, and one that focuses on "seeing the child." As white teachers, veteran and novice, we orient ourselves to these stories, these dominant narratives: we can embrace them or reject them—but they are always present, backdrops illuminating the relationships we forge between ourselves and our students.

But these stories, if they remain the only ones we know, sketch out impossibly narrow and regressive paths for white teachers. If we are to imagine other ways of configuring our teaching lives in opposition to white supremacy, we must find other stories—and we must find more nuanced meaning in the dominant stories that surround us. Nigerian novelist Chimamanda Adichie, in her powerful talk, "The Danger of a Single Story," points out:

It is impossible to talk about the single story without talking about power. There is a word, an Igbo word, that I think about whenever I think about the power structures of the world, and it is "nkali." It's a noun that loosely translates to "to be greater than another." Like our economic and political worlds, stories too are defined by the principle of nkali: How they are told, who tells them, when they're told, how many stories are told, are really dependent on power.

Power is the ability not just to tell the story of another person, but to make it the definitive story of that person (2007).

In this important book, Audrey Lensmire gives us some new stories to consider, and some insights into the old ones. She asks us to think about what it means to be a white teacher in a community of color, and, in doing so, outlines clearly the rigidity of the institution of schooling. Specifically, schooling is its own story, one that tells not only teachers who they are, but also students. In order to have new stories about white teachers, we have to also see and understand stories that may be new to us about students: their desire for achievement and belonging, their joy, their deep capacity.

Whether you are a new teacher, someone with years of experience, or a teacher educator, the stories collected here give you an opportunity to critically reflect on your own reality and context. No answers are given: like many parables, the point here is think about the meanings of these stories, how, in some instances, they reflect normative themes, the "single story" of white teachers, and how, in other instances, they offer paradoxes and new avenues for us to orient ourselves.

The difficulty of this task is the difficulty we have always had: how to think about our work and our lives in ways that don't make it all about the "us" of white teachers. How easy and simple it is to maintain a focus simply on why it's hard for white teachers in urban schools. Ultimately, however, this focus does nothing to imagine a practice of teaching that is engaged and radical. Recentering ourselves is an easy trap to fall into; all the more reason to engage critically, carefully, and courageously with what the teachers in this book are telling us.

Nikola Hobbel
Humboldt State University

Acknowledgments

This book has been in the making for a long time. It is with a deep sense of gratitude that I thank the teachers who agreed to tell their stories. Without you this book could not exist.

There have been a great many people who have supported me. To my colleagues Amanda Thein, Colleen Fairbanks, Lisa Albrecht, and Bic Ngo, thank you for helping me develop this work. To Rick Appelsies, thank you for the early years. Thank you to Cynthia Lewis, a mentor and friend, whose kind encouragement has kept me going. And, a special thank you to the Midwest Critical Whiteness Collective, Bryan Davis, Jessica Dockter, Mary Lee Nichols, Shannon McManimon, Tim Lensmire, and Zachary Casey, for your ongoing intellectual companionship.

It is perhaps impossible to thank my friends and family enough for their continued interest and encouragement in a seemingly interminable project such as this. So a big thank you to my lifelong friends Karyn Taeyaerts, Aimee Crow, Heather Ross, Amy McGinnis, and Kara Pacala and to my sisters Ellen Walthour, Jill Reister, and Joanne Brockington.

None of this would be possible without you, Tim. You are my inspiration. And you were right, this *is* what I wanted.

Introduction

When I was ten my father complained to me that he thought my sister and I were getting spoiled. My sister and I lived a white, middle-class life in the suburbs of Chicago with our mother. Dad decided to show us the way "it really was." I didn't know what *it* was until he took us for a drive to the south side and rambled on about how we were going to see "what *real life* is like."

My father was a talkative man and an expansive thinker. And, by that point in his life, he was suffering rather intensely from what today would be called bipolar disorder. His first breakdown was when he was a freshman at Brown in the late 1950s. He returned home and managed to graduate with a BS and an MBA from the University of Chicago. I'm not sure how he did this. In 2008, after he died, I found his transcripts. His grades were terrible.

In the early 1960s he met and married my mom: they had two kids and my mom thought she was set—a big house in the suburbs and a career man. A dozen years later my parents divorced. I grew up watching, feeling helpless as my father struggled with mania, depression, failed medications and hospitalizations, and then with loneliness, unemployment, homelessness, and poverty. It wasn't until the last decade of his life that he found something he always wanted: love. And because of this, because of Josephine, he enjoyed a kind of stability and sense of calm and purpose that had eluded him his whole life.

Throughout elementary school my sister and I spent weekends with him. It was on one of those days in 1979 that he drove us to the south side of Chicago where he grew up and had gone to school. Dad was proud of growing up and living in the city. The city was where "the action of life," as he put it, took place. The suburbs were anti-intellectual and materialistic.

On this particular day Dad drove and narrated us past his old house, through the university, and "deep into the heart of the city." He pointed out the many things that had changed, including the fact that there were more blacks in Hyde Park than when he was little. The story my father told us was that black people moved into the old neighborhood after his parents and other Jewish families "escaped" to the suburbs. He drove us up and down streets and alleys, slowing down by groups of black adults who were talking in small clusters in front of their houses.

I remember feeling afraid. My father's slow driving, his instructive chatter, his pointing out things from his past, created a sense of anxiety in me. Would he do something "weird" like stop the car, get out, and try to talk to people? Dad had the habit of talking to strangers everywhere—at the Laundromat, the pool, the hardware store, or the grocery. My sister and I were always mortified.

What I recall most is how small and white I felt. I stared out of the car window, slumped on the front seat next to my father. That encounter, with members of Chicago's black community, is forever mixed up with my worries about my father's talk, his habits and peculiar ways. I don't remember him saying anything to suggest that I should fear black people. After all, he wanted to show us what "life was really like," which included first, that people of color existed, and second, that poor people, like him, existed.

An expansive sense of what was normal, of what it meant to be human, began to grow inside of me. It was possible to become spoiled by living a middle-class life in the suburbs, if it meant (and I think it did) that that way of living was thought of as right, normal, desirable, attainable. My dad, both consciously and unconsciously, taught me that there were and are multiple ways of living and being in the world. Those early experiences with Dad played a large part in shaping my deepest commitments, my deepest concerns.

In my early twenties I became a teacher. Like many people who go into teaching, I thought it would be a way to make a difference in the world. My first job was at an urban middle school in Austin, Texas, teaching language arts to Mexican American and African American young people. During that first year I taught one white student and for the next five years mine was the only white face in the classroom.

The daily work of teaching provided an opening for relationships with people of color (students, colleagues, and families) that was new for me. I felt prepared and exhilarated by the students and the work we shared. There were also times when it seemed impossible to teach kids whose racial and cultural backgrounds and life experiences were so different than mine.

I witnessed violence, the absurd. Early in my first year of teaching, I watched a veteran white teacher throw a Mexican American sixth grader (a little kid) against a wall and tell him "You are going to end up in jail if you don't shape up." She explained to me that "these kids need to hear the truth." A few years later she became the assistant principal. Then I taught in another public school. The students wore uniforms and were taught to walk in lines with their hands held behind their backs. The students were African American, the teachers and administrators overwhelmingly white. The school was nicknamed "The Plantation" by the surrounding community.

These moments (and so many others) were difficult for me, but what made it worse was that there was no talk, no discussion, no explicit and honest sense-making about what this was all about. What we as white teachers were up to, why it was so hard, why things seemed so wrong. I talked with colleagues—we stole moments of confusion and frustration around the edges of our work. But there was no official time to talk about how race and poverty and schooling were all mixed up. How we were too often failing to educate our students.

I went to graduate school to try to make some sense out of my teaching experiences and questions about race and school. As a teacher, I had only scratched the surface of the ways that race makes up the very fabric of our society and our individual lives. As I studied, I came in contact with scholars, social commentators, and literary writers who thought and wrote about race. [1]

As I worked to understand race, its practices and its complicated intersections with schooling, I was persuaded by Gloria Ladson-Billings and William Tate's (1995), insistence, with reference to Marcus Garvey's writings, on a "race-first" perspective in education. A "race-first" perspective could, they argued, move the K–12 educational system toward equity for students of color (I discuss some of the problems with a white person taking up a race-first perspective in the Appendix).

Because I was curious about how experienced white urban teachers would narrate their work lives and because I wanted to sort through how a race-first theory of education could help explain white teachers' experiences and feelings about race, I decided to undertake an interview project. I conducted one initial and one follow-up ethnographic, biographical interview with five white teachers—each of them having worked in urban schools for more than five years. [2]

Inspired by Kathleen Casey's (1993) research on the lives of women teachers, the first interview was structured around one question: "Tell me the story of your work as a white teacher." [3] "Story" signaled to the participants that I was actually interested in their stories: that is, that they did not need to analyze their experiences or have "answers" as to what their stories might mean, racially or otherwise.

I purposely used the word "white" as a signal that I wanted to hear stories about race from their perspectives as white teachers, as racialized people working with children of color in urban schools. In the second interview, each teacher and I reviewed a transcription of the first interview that I had prepared. I asked questions about things I did not understand. Many of these interviews had the feel of a conversation.

These interviews generated stories, dozens of them. These stories were socially produced ways of recalling and retelling experiences. Here, they are re-presented and interpreted as embedded within larger social, historical, and political narratives of school, equity, hope, and critique. In the following chapters I read these stories in relation to theories of race and racism in order to illuminate what it means to be a white teacher.

There were many similarities among the teachers' experiences. It would have been easy to identify common themes and to create a simple narrative, perhaps entitled "The Story of White Urban Teachers."

This simple narrative would go as follows: First, as beginning white teachers, they struggled to manage their classroom, to control their students, and to implement the curriculum with a modicum of success. They learned to build relationships with peers and to communicate with families and the administration. After several years, they decided to focus on building relationships with their students. They figured out that this was key to being able to teach. They worried less about the official curriculum and more about individual students' needs. They gained confidence. On some days they thought they did a good job. Eventually, they found themselves completely engaged. They felt as though there was no place that they would rather be working than with students of color in urban schools.

I could have told that story (and it might be an important one). But then, how would the reader understand the fears Charlotte experienced, not only as a new teacher, but even in talking with me, her friend, about race? When would the reader learn about Darrin and his complicated, tragic relationship with his brilliant student, Antonio, a relationship that seemed to repeat centuries-old power relations between white and black men? And Paul, Frida, and Margaret—these teachers cared for and about their students, but saying they cared would provide readers little insight into the divergent desires that motivated this care. Therefore, the idea of trying to tell a story of their similarities was abandoned.

These stories, in their original tellings and in my subsequent retellings and interpretations, complicate previously held ideas about the lives of white teachers working with students of color in urban schools. Each participant— Charlotte, Darrin, Paul, Frida, and Margaret—had important and different things to teach us.[4]

Chapter 1 frames the questions that drove the research and writing of this book. In it I pay particular attention to how racial categories function to both illuminate and obscure the experiences of white teachers. I provide a short examination of what race is and how it came to matter in the United States. I

discuss work on whiteness in education with help from Gloria Ladson-Billings and William Tate and others, in order to attend to the intersections of
race, whiteness, and education.

Then, drawing heavily on the work on white racial identity by the Reverend Thandeka, I underscore her theorization of how white adults thwart the
"natural" impulses of their children to seek cross-racial relationships. Thandeka's work on "white shame" was particularly important and I draw on it in
later chapters.

Finally, I discuss current research on race and education and teacher
education. I argue that while there is much to learn from whiteness studies in
education, the problem remains that we do not yet have a body of compelling
research that studies white teachers as racialized beings.

Chapter 2 traces an interview with Charlotte, and how it became clear that
she was uncomfortable talking about her work. Despite our past history
together (as teacher colleagues and friends) and our desire to talk with each
other about race and education, we struggled to find a way to explore significant aspects of our experiences. This chapter moves through interrelated
stories, exploring two main themes—racial fears and white shame. Charlotte's stories challenged images from research and popular culture of the
"good white activist" and challenged the image of who would be considered
a "good white teacher."

Chapter 3 is about Darrin, an English and theater teacher with a terrific
ability to tell stories. The chapter opens with a look at the beginning of
Darrin's teaching career and his assumption that he would always (as an
adult and a teacher) be treated with respect. He described his early teaching
as a "nightmare" and found himself thinking of some students as "unteachable."

He narrated how his own racial self-concept shifted radically as he
watched his black students' responses to the O. J. Simpson verdict: "It was
really apparent to me that there was a lot I did not understand about race."

Much of this chapter centers on tracing and interpreting his tragic relationship with his student, Antonio. Two stories, which I named "Fire and
Ice" and "The Kiss," explored the ways that Darrin and Antonio—as teacher
and student, as white man and black adolescent—struggled for power, dis-
rupted school norms, and found fleeting moments of mastery and control.

I interpreted what happened between Darrin and Antonio by connecting
the stories to larger histories of colonialism, white male supremacy, and
heteronormativity, and explored how these legacies find their ways into our
schools, classrooms, and teacher/student relationships.

Chapter 4 develops three interrelated themes in relation to Paul, Frida,
and Margaret and their experiences: (1) white teachers' desires, (2) the complexities of caring in schools, and (3) the difficulties of reading white teachers' stories. First, I share a story from my own life—an account of what I

thought it meant to be a good white activist. This story enabled me to begin an exploration of how white teachers (and the researchers who study them) often misread who they are as racial actors in schools.

For example, Paul's ability to "see the child" helped him find ways to connect students and families with whom he worked. It did not, however, keep racist thoughts from bubbling up from time to time. Frida sought work at an urban school because she wanted her work to have meaning, to "be genuinely involved in humanity." Frida changed her speech and dress out of a desire to be "more than just another white woman" to her African American students. Margaret's story was of place and agency, and of desire—a wish, a wondering about how her work might be different if she were black.

Chapter 5 concludes my book and reflects how the stories in the previous chapters allow readers to think in more expansive ways about who white urban teachers are and who they can become as they engage in teaching with children and families of color in urban communities.

I have included an appendix of research methods for those who might be interested in how I conducted the study and how I wrote and interpreted the stories. One methodological note: I chose to avoid creating an organizing system ("categories") or a way of comparing the teachers to each other because I was on the lookout for differences in relation to commonly held beliefs about white teachers. Instead, I worked to make sense out of the emotional, personal experience of being white, of being a teacher, and of being a white teacher.

The stories in this book are about the work of being a white teacher in urban schools. They are stories of fear and loss, control and authority, and care and desire. Their labor was a complex, hard, and joyful struggle to teach children of color in spite of the tidal wave of racial history, politics, economics, and language that repeatedly conspired to overwhelm them. I don't write this story as a defense of their efforts. At times, their beliefs and actions were misguided and did damage to those in their care. They, and we, have much to learn.

Each teacher was, in their own way, a thoughtful human being committed to being a good teacher of urban students. This way of being, of living, of teaching, is a lifelong process, wrapped up with moral commitments and political implications. This book looks broadly at questions of human relationship and the work of teaching and learning. What is it that is worthy in how we live our lives and do our work with others? How do we work to become the kind of people who live up to ideals of social justice, democracy, community, and freedom?

We need to open ourselves again to stories—hearing them afresh and interpreting them anew and finding in them the necessary critique and hope to move forward in our efforts for social justice and humane schooling practices.

I wrote this book for teachers who know that this life of teaching is, all the time, full of paradoxes, complexities, and struggles. I wrote this book also for teacher educators who have in them a nagging sense that there is more to explore with their education students about what it means to become a white teacher in twenty-first-century America. This book, I hope, can open up new spaces for more complex and nuanced conversations about race, teaching, and whiteness.

NOTES

1. The body of work that ultimately persuaded me of the centrality of race was the historical documentation of race-making. I learned that around the world, throughout modern times, the darker one's skin color, the fewer chances he or she has to live peacefully and in relative prosperity. During the "Age of Reason," for example, scientists measured, classified, and ranked human species. The making of these hierarchies, based upon head size and other physical characteristics, is, for me, some of the most damaging work that has been done in the name of science. These classifications sound ridiculous now when said out loud—human beings were rank ordered by skin color and appearance with the best, the lightest, on top. The worst part is that these rankings ultimately shaped the way American society was formed and transformed throughout the years. Race continues to matter.

2. See the appendix for a lengthier discussion of the research method.

3. Using one framing question for an interview is called a "biographic-narrative interview," in which the researcher's "contribution is limited to a single question (aimed at inducing narrative) and in which all of your other interventions are reduced to a minimum and drained of any particular content " (Wengraf 2001, 113).

4. All teachers and schools named in the text are pseudonyms.

Chapter One

Race and Education

To be human today is to be raced. —john powell

This book is grounded in historical accounts of race, critical race theory in education, and research about white teachers. Research and writings on race, racial categories, structural and personal racism, whiteness, white privilege, race in schooling, and race at its intersections with class, ethnicity, language, and capitalism are voluminous.

The aim of this chapter is to provide a backdrop for the questions that drove the research and writing of this book, and to help contextualize the teacher stories in the next three chapters. Particular attention was paid to how racial categories function—in part because a primary purpose of this research was to expand the boundaries that categories create. The chapter opens with a description of what race is and how it came to matter in the United States, and moves to a discussion of research about the development of white identity and how white teachers have been conceptualized in educational research.

RACE AND RACIAL CATEGORIES: A MODERN INVENTION

David Theo Goldberg (1993) argued that the central work of modernity (1500s to the present) has been to order and to classify people, to create and to maintain hierarchies. Goldberg wrote,

> Sufficiently broad, indeed, almost conceptually empty, race offers itself as a category capable of providing a semblance of social cohesion, of historical particularity, of given meanings and motivations to agents. (p. 4)

1

The concept of race and the way that race is done in the United States was an invention of modernity, consistent with its need for order and measure (Goldberg 1993; Hannaford 1995).

Race has remained an organizing principle of our nation (Mills 1997; Omi and Winant 1994; Roediger 2000; Takaki 2000). That is to say, that because race—erroneously (tragically) was thought to be biologically, "scientifically" true, it was used to sort people and determine their place and worth in society. Race, though "almost conceptually empty," defined, shaped, and continues to define and shape the experiences of both people of color and white people.

History is rife with examples of how this defining occurred (Omi and Winant 1994; Roediger 2000). The late Ronald Takaki (2000) carefully traced how, during the 1800s, whites came to believe that blacks deserved their low status. Blacks were thought of as childlike, savage, and uneducable when compared to white adult men. Whites valued being a civilized, rational, and homogenous people (Takaki 2000, p. 12).

Materially speaking, "White over black had an organic relationship to class divisions and conflicts forming within white society" (Takaki 2000, p. 127). Takaki and others have argued that the desire and successful accumulation of material dominance by white elites fractured any possibility of solidarity between the new working-class whites and blacks, all but ensuring oppression of people of color.

Psychologically speaking, white elites did not gain power and riches without regret: they longed for a freer, less time-structured existence than they remembered before they became progress-oriented capitalists. David Roediger's (2000) seminal work demonstrated how whites "longed" for aspects of themselves they had given up.

> Racism grew so strongly among the Anglo-American bourgeoisie during the years America was colonized because blackness came to symbolize that which the accumulating capitalist had given up, but still longed for. Increasingly adopting an ethos that attacked holidays, spurned contact with nature, saved time, bridled sexuality, separated work from the rest of life and postponed gratification, profit-minded Englishmen and Americans cast Blacks as their former selves. . . . All of the old habits so recently discarded by whites adopting capitalist values came to be fastened onto Blacks. (p. 95)

White elites and white workers' new work discipline and "capitalist values" engendered a romantic notion of a freer past and contempt for those who were imagined to represent it. As Takaki (2000) noted, "one of the surest ways to confirm an identity, for communities as well as for individuals, is to find some way of measuring *what one is not*" (italics in original, p. 33).

People of color have always understood this social and political organization (Mills 1997). Simultaneously, white people have *not* understood the "centrality of race." Mills explained,

> Nonwhites then find that race is, paradoxically, both everywhere and nowhere, structuring their lives but not formally recognized in political/moral theory. But in a racially structured polity, the only people who can find it psychologically possible to deny the centrality of race are those who are racially privileged, for whom race is invisible precisely because the world is structured around them, whiteness as the ground against which the figures of other races—those who unlike us, are raced—appear. The fish does not see the water, and whites do not see the racial nature of a white polity because it is natural to them. (p. 76)

There is much that can be said of Mills' racial contract but I want to emphasize three points: (1) our society is ordered by race; (2) one privilege of being white is the ability to deny that race orders things; and (3) being white seems normal (and better) and therefore everything else seems to be different (and worse).

Today, whiteness is conceptualized as a vast culture of power and privilege and the unexamined position of the majority (McLaren 1998; Essed and Goldberg 2002). For many, whiteness has probably been described best as "unattainable property" (Harris 1995). Critical race theorists, whose work is rooted in legal history, take up how taken-for-granted notions about social phenomenon were in fact "subtly intertwined" with race and racism (Essed and Goldberg 2002). Analytically, it is possible to look at how "all variations on and through 'race' serve as codes and manifestations of power more generally" (Essed and Goldberg 2002, p. 4).

Critical race theory and historical accounts have provided powerful frameworks for analytical work about white lives. Racial categories provided a useful starting point for research about white teachers. However, white teachers' work experiences, feelings, and thoughts cannot only be examined from within categories.

Caroline Knowles (2003) understood this. The relationship, she wrote, between the category and the self is worthy of exploration.

> Racial categories, I had started to see, obscure hugely divergent social positions, which could be unpacked and mapped onto (an interpretation of) the social fabric as something composed of different kinds of racialized lives. That there are differences within social categories is a banal and unsurprising insight; that difference can offer a starting point in a more detailed account of the operation of race and the racial texture of society is actually rather exciting. (p. 23)

Knowles' claim, that there are "different kinds of racialized lives," was a premise of this study. In other words, I expected that the interviews would uncover different kinds of white lives.

WHITE LIVES

But how do white people become white in the first place? The Reverend Thandeka's (1999) theorization of the genesis of white identity has been crucial to my understanding of the violence of race, even for white people. She asserted that there is a violent and harmful process involved in "becoming" white; a process that involves the abuse of white children by their own white community.

Thandeka thought that white children's experiences with white authority taught them, in effect, how to be white. For Thandeka, white children learn, often in subtle and implicit ways, that attraction to people who are outside the white community is wrong. White children learn that they should not desire or love people who are not white.

Furthermore, they learn that they may lose the love and support of their own parents and community if they persist in being attracted to or in love with people who are not white. Thandeka theorized that white racial identity is wrapped up with a deep *shame* that is created when "prewhite" children learn that there is something wrong with them, deep inside; and what is "wrong" with them is that they have desires that exceed their own racial community.

Thandeka's work on "white shame" was important to my thinking about white identity and for my work with the white teachers in this study. She theorized that white children become white adults with a deep, unnamed confusion and shame about issues related to race (Lensmire 2010, p. 167). Thandeka's work helped me listen to and be compassionate toward my participants.

I never lost sight of the fact that they were adults—adults who had power and responsibility in relation to their students of color. At the same time, they were also former white children who became confused, ambivalent, and difference-fearing adults. I turned to Thandeka's work many times during the writing of this book to understand my participants' stories.

WHITE TEACHERS IN SCHOOLS

Schools are places that exemplify white norms and middle-class values despite social activism and counterhegemonic discourse (Sleeter 1996; Thompson 2001). Policies and practices of urban bureaucratic school systems privilege white norms (Banks and Banks 1997; Britzman 1986; Cochran-Smith 1995; Delpit 1995; Kailin 1999; Kincheloe et al. 1998; Sleeter 1993, 1996).

While it is true that schools are nestled within larger social, economic, and political cultures, some educators have taken up the problems of race and whiteness in their work with future and practicing teachers in hopes of dismantling the curricular practices of schools and teachers that reify white norms (Ladson-Billings 1994, 2001; Kumashiro 2004). Intervening in the education of future teachers, who are typically white, middle-class, young women, is critically important.

Educational research and popular discourse figure white teachers in either one of two ways: as the object of our hope or of our disdain. We hope that white teachers are able to successfully educate children of color. We hope that white teachers are serious enough, smart enough, caring enough to refuse the damaging stereotypes of children of color. We hope that white teachers challenge their students of color to become adults who will claim powerful roles in our democracy.

We loathe white teachers too. We fear that they have contributed to the stubborn achievement gap because of their personal failures. After all, they work in American public schools. White teachers are key players in a public institution that has a long history of policies and practices that have held back children of color and children from poor families from realizing their highest potential.

Scholars of color have long been writing about issues of race and (in)equity in education. James Banks is credited with bringing multicultural education to the fore. Gloria Ladson-Billings' classic *Dreamkeepers: Successful Teachers of African-American Children* (1994) focused on characteristics of effective teachers of African American students. The teachers profiled in her book were, significantly, both black and white. Lisa Delpit's *Other People's Children: Cultural Conflict in the Classroom* (1995) had much to say to progressive white teachers about their obligation to instruct students of color about how to access the culture of power. Sonia Nieto's *The Light in Their Eyes: Creating Multicultural Learning Communities* addressed all teachers who wished to positively impact the lives of diverse students. I share in the hopes that these esteemed scholars convey that not only is it possible for white teachers to teach students of color well, it is necessary.

Research on white teachers has documented how white teachers were unaware, at times, of race altogether (Marx 2001; McIntyre 1997); were resistant to learning about race and racism (Sleeter 1993); defended white privilege (Kailin 1999; Marx 2001; McIntyre 1997); and named the ways in which they benefited from being white (Marx 2001; Trepagnier 2001).

Research has also demonstrated how white preservice teachers conceptualized working in urban areas (McIntyre 1997); how in-service teachers worked to make curriculum meaningful for students of color (Ladson-Billings 1994; Landsman 2001); and how some teacher-educators attempted to teach preservice white teachers about whiteness (Sleeter 1993). The intention, I believe, of this body of work was to illuminate the powerful ways in which whiteness operates in schools and to reveal strategies that teacher-educators can use to teach ways of interrupting what has become commonly called the "achievement gap."

Four carefully rendered studies on whiteness and white racial identity were especially important to this study. The purpose of studies of white teachers is not to recenter white people, to reassert their ways of being as normal, as desirable, as right. Instead, the purpose of studies such as these is to better understand the insidious ways in which race, whiteness, and power manifest themselves and to use this information to make change.

Alice McIntyre (1997) sought to actively involve herself with thirteen white preservice teachers in an exploration of racial identity. She wanted to look at whiteness from the inside, as it was lived, reflected upon, and explained by the white women who participated in her study.

McIntyre was particularly disturbed by her research participants' reliance on what she called "white talk":

> Talk that serves to insulate white people from examining their/our individual and collective role(s) in the perpetuation of racism. It is a result of whites talking uncritically with/to other whites, all the while resisting critique and massaging each other's racist attitudes, beliefs, and actions. (p. 46)

White talk made it difficult for McIntyre to intervene pedagogically with her students.

McIntyre's participants constructed whiteness positively. They portrayed white people as "living a fairy tale" and as "keepers of the American Dream" (p. 79). Several of McIntyre's participants discovered and acknowledged that whiteness is the "norm" of this society. For example, one participant noted that as whites "we don't have anything to prove," and another added that you don't even "have to think about it" (p. 86).

When the participants began to understand racism more fully, they quickly defined themselves as "good whites" against others who were "bad whites." Good whites are not racist. Bad whites are.

Barbara Trepagnier's (2001) studied twenty-five white women who self-identified as good white people, as "not racist." Her analysis of the women's talk and writing demonstrated what she called their "silent racism." She found that the women relied on stereotypical images and paternalistic assumptions in relation to people of color.

> Stereotypical images concerning black Americans refers to the misinformation and false images learned informally by white Americans and that distinguish blacks as "different." Paternalistic assumptions refer to a condescending attitude toward blacks characterized by a sense of false responsibility. (p. 149)

These findings were evident *despite* the women's desires and beliefs that they were "not racist."

Trepagnier argued that—while we might believe that we are not racist, that we are good people and that we work, at times, against racism—we retain "misinformation and false images" of blacks and consequently hold a "sense of false responsibility" toward them. Trepagnier's study helped me understand how "good white" teachers can simultaneously be well intentioned with students of color *and* behave in racist and harmful ways.

Jennifer Seibel Trainor (2002) warned that critical educational scholars and activists sometimes participate in sorting out good and bad white people, as if that is the important thing to do. She worried that, too often, we tell stories in which we position ourselves as the good white people against the bad white people who are our students and research participants. "We" are the antiracist teachers and researchers and "they" are not; we are the stuff of moral agency and are on the right path; they are racist and politically unaware. As Trainor (2002) put it: "Racism, classism, sexism, domination, injustice are critical pedagogy's necessary other. But seeming perpetrators of this other often sit in our classrooms" (p. 636).

Sherry Marx (2001) did research with her own students, white preservice teachers who were tutoring students of color. Marx's writing showed both sensitivity and respect toward her participants, especially in how she refused to separate herself from them. Her research illuminated several important dimensions of whiteness that were evidenced in her participants' stories about their work with children of color.

Like other studies and writing about white teachers (Cochran-Smith 1995; Delpit 1995), Marx's participants associated students of color with deficits of culture, language, family life, self-esteem, or intelligence. The future teachers Marx studied expressed fear of people of color; viewed themselves as role models; believed they were, as white educators, natural saviors of children whose lives they imagined as "miserable"; and suggested that their tutoring was simply charity work that was rewarding to perform (Marx 2001). These findings were both troubling and instructive as to the critical need to intervene in the education of future teachers.

Marx simultaneously took up the role of university supervisor for the students and researcher. It was in the writing up of her findings that she reinforced her connection to them.

> The stories participants and I shared marked our own places in time and space (Freire 1970/2000). That is, they situated us as humans socialized by our lifetimes in the later 20th and early 21st centuries, the places we grew up, the families and friends who nurtured us, and, necessarily, the Whiteness and racism that characterize our privileged status in the United States. In this study, our stories constructed and then conveyed our realities. (p. 34)

Using storytelling humanized Marx's work and relationship to her research participants. It was because of Marx that I was persuaded that it would be possible to retell white teachers' stories in ways that conveyed my connection to and respect for them and still pay attention to troubling aspects of white racial identities and racism.

CONCLUSION

Racial categories cannot contain all that we need to know about white people's lives. Racial categories still offered a useful starting point for research. One reason for pursuing the idea of whiteness was not because white teachers have not been the objects, subjects, and participants in educational research. They are, in fact, the very teachers upon which we have based educational research. The problem is that we do not yet have a body of compelling research that studies teachers as white, racialized beings. In this specific manner, race has long been ignored.

With the dangers of pursuing this kind of work in mind, I remained curious about the ways in which working white teachers' identities are constructed and reconstructed amidst their work with students of color in urban schools. Tensions and contradictions arise *among* white people with the living that accompanies teaching. Tensions and contradictions arise for white people *in our insides* too.

White identity is not just one thing—not just an unexamined and privileged way of living. As the philosopher Maxine Greene (1995) explained, "Neither my self or my narrative can have a single strand. I stand at the crossing point of too many social and cultural forces; I am forever on the way" (p. 1).

Amy Winans (2005) observed that all people have "contradictory experiences." The "broad narratives" we know about race do not adequately (or completely) allow us to understand the "complexities of race in people's lived experiences."

> Indeed, many of the current approaches to whiteness and white students create obstacles to developing effective pedagogies, ones that allow students to explore the complex, often contradictory experiences that are obscured by the broad narratives that they are frequently encouraged to adopt when they do talk about race in their lives. The difficulty that emerges in recent scholarship on whiteness and pedagogies of whiteness is not unlike that encountered by many white students in or from predominantly white areas: similar narratives are repeated, yet they efface the complexities of race in people's lived experiences and the role that emotions play in one's understanding of those experiences. (p. 73)

That is, race shapes our social relationships, our struggles toward our collective and individual notions of who we are existentially, both in spite of and to spite the abstractions that describe our experiences. Human beings are constantly working, in-relationship, struggling on multiple levels, in order to work out identities, our places in the world, our ways of being.

Despite knowing about our race history and racial categories, I was left with questions of how individuals act and react to a structure that seemed deterministic. That is, if we are all actors in a racialized culture where does that leave the intimacy of human interactions? How can history help us make sense out of today's human interactions and human relationships?

In the three chapters that follow, you will hear from and come to know the work lives of five white teachers: Charlotte, Darrin, Paul, Frida, and Margaret. The stories they told offered new ways of thinking about what it means to be a white teacher working with students of color in urban schools.

Chapter Two

Charlotte's Losses: Racial Fears and White Shame

Charlotte's story was like the stories of many white urban teachers. As white teachers cross into the nonwhite zones[1] of urban classrooms in communities of color, they also cross into unknown zone inside themselves. These inside zones are part of what white teachers must navigate as they work to become the kind of teachers they had hoped to become.

This chapter moves through two interrelated stories, namely: (1) Charlotte's account of her work life and (2) her account of becoming a white teacher. Charlotte and I learned, together, that there were important things that could be learned by talking explicitly about race. At the same time, we learned that it was hard to talk explicitly about race, despite our years of friendships and work together. My writing in this chapter moves like my conversations with Charlotte—in circles within circles—as I retell and interpret Charlotte's stories.

CHARLOTTE'S WORK LIFE

Charlotte has a classic Scandinavian appearance—white-blond hair, light blue eyes, and fair white skin. We met after we were both hired in 1996 to teach at a new urban elementary school on the north side of this city. We started talking on the phone during the early evening as we each prepared dinner. During these conversations we told each other about our day and tried to make sense out of the things that had happened.

We were and continue to be confidantes. We were nevertheless amazed to see how this research opened new spaces, even for old friends. At first, Charlotte was a practice interviewee. She had agreed to help me figure out if the idea I had for a research project would work. Ultimately, I included her stories because they were compelling—revealing much about race, whiteness, fear, loss, *and* care.

Like each of the subsequent research participants, Charlotte needed confirmation at the outset of our first interview. We sat at her kitchen table with the tape recorder between us. She earnestly wanted to help me. First, she wanted to make sure she had the question right.

> I thought about it a little since we talked on Friday and, since I tend to overanalyze things, I ended up thinking I guess my story as a white teacher isn't necessarily different than my story as a teacher. I was trying to think of what you were asking me to think about. And so my assessment is that you wanted to know more about my experience as a teacher, related to me being white, working with students of color and what that experience has been like for me since I began.

Charlotte's understanding of what I had asked her to do was correct. I wanted to know more about her experiences as a white teacher. And it seemed, at least at first, that for her *that* story was not different than her story of being a teacher. But she was not sure. She tried to sort it out.

> So that brought me to thinking about how I began [teaching] and how did I end up being a white teacher? Because I wasn't a white teacher until I worked with students of color. Do you know what I mean? I don't think I felt like a white teacher. I don't think I felt like that meant anything until I was at Mercer, and maybe that's because that's my real first year of teaching. That was the first time I felt like a real teacher.

Charlotte wasn't a white teacher until she was in the presence of students of color during her "first real year of teaching." In her first classroom at Mercer, when she realized that she was the ultimate authority in the classroom—in charge, in control, and responsible for teaching well—that was when she became a real white teacher.

Charlotte's college experiences pulled her in the direction of working with students of color. It might not have been an explicit part of her teacher-education program but, like many education students, Charlotte was placed in a tutoring role with English language learners. Twice a week she went to a local high school and tutored a student from China. The next semester she became the tutoring trainer, supervising and observing other tutors.

The tutoring was "a really good experience" that caused Charlotte to request a student-teaching placement in the city with English language learners. After graduation she was hired as a resident teacher at Circle Pines Elementary, an urban school with a high percentage of students of color. In many ways being a resident teacher was like being an apprentice. Charlotte was part of an experienced team of teachers, not responsible for her own class but an integral part of planning curriculum and working with students. It was a pivotal year for her.

> I was fortunate to work with a team of three teachers who were effective and were happy to be teaching where they were teaching and to be teaching who they were teaching. That really gave me an opportunity to see something positive going on in a learning setting for students of color. I think that's really important because when I think about things that I've seen going on in learning settings for students of color that aren't good, where I see them not being happy in the classroom or I perceive them as not being happy in the classroom, that makes me really sad and I know that it doesn't have to be that way because I've seen it other ways.

Charlotte was led into urban teaching in positive ways. She worked one-on-one with English language learners as a tutor, had an influential professor for a diversity course, and was surrounded by teachers who were "happy to be teaching where they were teaching and to be teaching who they were teaching." The "where" and "who" in the above excerpt were white teachers teaching students of color in an urban school.

Despite these positive first experiences with students of color, Charlotte was afraid of having her own classroom the following fall at Mercer Elementary. The morning of our first interview, Charlotte and her family had been at church. The minister spoke about fear in terms of current events in the Middle East, unemployment, and fear in general in people's lives. Reflecting on the sermon and thinking of our upcoming meeting Charlotte said she was:

> thinking about whether or not fear defines our experiences about things, or to what degree does fear define our experiences in life, professionally and personally and otherwise. I was thinking about as a new teacher, what was I afraid of? I always think about myself at Mercer because that's where I spent the most time and felt the most invested, so that's where I picture myself when I reflect. So I was thinking, what were my fears?

Charlotte's question, "What were my fears?" might have been rhetorical at first but functioned to open a space for her to name the fears she felt as a new teacher.

My fears were that the discipline would just be out of control and kids would be hurting each other and yelling and horrible things going on like that. And my fears were that their parents wouldn't accept me, or that I would get the blank stare and I wouldn't be able to connect with them when they were talking about their child and how they were doing in school. Or that they wouldn't know I had their best interests in mind and in heart for their children. And they wouldn't believe in it and then we couldn't work together. That we would have a lot of barriers there and I couldn't be as successful as I wanted to be. I had fears about that my students wouldn't learn from me as much as I wanted them to. Then when I felt like they did really well with me, I had fears of them going on to a new teacher.

Charlotte shared a litany of fears. On the surface Charlotte's fears—of not being in control, not being seen as both authoritative and compassionate—were typical of new teachers. Yet, I couldn't help but wonder about the ways in which race played a part in all of it.

During our second interview, we returned together to examine the list of her fears about teaching. I wanted to know if the fears she had as a first year teacher were related to race. Were the "barriers" she talked about related to racial difference, racial tension, or racial politics?

A: And I even want to just push you even more. Because you said in the beginning when you were a teacher you were anxious.

C: Uh huh.

A: And I just want to ask you again were you anxious because there was racial—

C: Yeah.

A: Ok.

C: Uh huh.

A quiet and thoughtful woman, Charlotte did not typically interrupt, as she did here in the middle of my question. When she listed her fears about teaching, she had said nothing about race. Her interruption, however, became the moment of recognition of what had been unsaid. It provided an opening for us to talk about how race and fears had become intertwined. We pushed on into the unknown territory of talking about racial fears together.

A: Can you talk about anxiety related to race?

C: Well part of it is, I guess, anxiety related to race is, I didn't know anything about black people when I started teaching. I really have had very few black friends in my life, not because I haven't chosen them I just haven't had access. You know I just haven't been around people of color. Hadn't been until college, really. I mean, some, but not like as the two white people in the room of twenty-six people.

When Charlotte had the responsibility of her own classroom (not a tutor, not a resident teacher), when she entered a nonwhite zone, she had to consider how much she didn't know about people of color. Charlotte grew up in a mostly white suburb, lived in an urban area for a few years, and returned to the suburbs to raise her children.

When she first began teaching African American students, Charlotte felt "anxious" and "uneasy." It wouldn't necessarily have seemed that way from the outside. Charlotte was known as a caring teacher, the teacher in the building who actually knew all of the students by name. Two things were worth noting in the following excerpt—how she thought of being in relationship with people and how her lack of experiences with people of color affected her. Charlotte explained her unease:

> I didn't know anything about their lives, their culture, their families. I didn't know anybody personally, intimately, or how they felt. Hadn't helped anybody when they were sad or, you know, had anybody share feelings with me or their thoughts and so that made me uneasy because. . . . Why did that make me uneasy? I don't know.

On the one hand, it seemed sensitive for Charlotte to admit that people of another race and culture need to be experienced in order to be known. Without "knowing anybody personally," it was hard for Charlotte to feel at ease with her black students and their families.

On the other hand, her not knowing anything about "*their* lives, *their* culture, about *their* families" was a form of Othering.[2] Why would she assume that *these* people have lives, culture, and families that were so different than her own? But Charlotte's initial fears, anxiety, and unease changed as her confidence in her teaching grew and she had positive experiences with her students.

At the time of our interviews, Charlotte had moved on from Mercer Elementary and was working as a "gifted and talented" teacher in another urban neighborhood that was primarily white and upper-middle class. She drew some strong contrasts between her former students of color and her new white students.

Charlotte missed her old students. She missed the intensity of the relation-ships, the ups and downs of her students' moods, and the closeness she felt with her peers. There was, as she put it, an "emotional connection" with her students that she missed. Charlotte admitted that she might be "romanticiz-ing" a bit, but she felt quite sad about leaving Mercer.

> I think I felt like my kids at Mercer more had their heart on their sleeve. And it just allowed me to get to know them better. I could see their sense of humor. Their sense of humor was present. I mean the walls were up too. I don't know, I guess I feel like I'm going in circles.

Charlotte knew her students—recognizing both their emotional openness *and* their emotional walls. Yet, her thinking in "circles" was confusing.

Charlotte was attracted to the emotional vulnerability of her African American students. There was something special, something *different* about their humor and their walls that she felt captured by, drawn toward. She *longed* for that type of connection again because she felt it was absent in her relationships with white students. Not only did she sense her African American students needed her (a sort of savior mentality, perhaps), but she found she needed them too.

Thandeka (1999) suggested that we might think of "longings" and "at-traction" as emotions that cover "feelings of dismay, distress, loss, rage, and anger at one's own white environment because it prevented the self from retaining a fuller and more inclusive range of its own sentient feelings" (p. 75).

It was possible that once Charlotte engaged in the literal and figurative nonwhite zone and experienced the "Other," she realized that she had lost (or never had) something important. In becoming white, while working with students of color, she had experienced a "more inclusive range" of feelings than she had previously known in her all-white communities.

Charlotte's reflections reminded me of Todd DeStigter's (2001) observa-tion about white people working in communities of color.

> It is good that we hesitate at *fronteras* of ethnicity, gender, language, and social class. We have ample reason to pause and wonder whether we should take that next step and presume to participate in the lives of others. (italics in original, p. 313)

Perhaps without knowing it, Charlotte had hesitated along the *fronteras* of race and social class. And she decided along the way, consciously or not, to "take that next step."

The border of her youth and inexperience also caused some hesitation. Charlotte said it was not the students she was afraid of, but rather, their parents. She was afraid of not connecting with them and not being effective.

> I guess at some level I must have had an awareness that there was potentially a distrust of white people by some of the parents or a distrust of the school system. I must have learned or read something along the way where I knew school might not seem like a friendly place to families of color.

Charlotte connected her own self-consciousness and fears to a tentative recognition of the experiences of some African American parents and their potential "distrust of the school system." Unlike the experienced teachers in Kailnin's (1999) study who blamed individual students of color for school discipline problems, or McIntyre's (1997) participants' "white talk" that "constructed barriers to fully grasping the racial hierarchy that exists in the United States" (p. 61), Charlotte knew there was a system at work that was not hospitable to families of color.

Charlotte moved into more specific talk about race, so I asked her directly if her fears about "discipline" were about racial stereotypes of black urban youth being resistant learners and disrespectful of teachers. In our first interview Charlotte had said this did not have to do with race. But with the benefit of time and thought, Charlotte admitted that her fears about student behavior might have had "racial roots."

> There might have been some fear about if somebody might have access to a weapon at home and might bring it to school or something like that, which might have had racial roots in my mind. Just because of stereotypes again, and thinking that there are guns in people's homes. And there are in white people's homes too, but guns on the streets and stuff like that.

Over time Charlotte's fears subsided. She never had any real experiences that may have contributed to or confirmed her fears. Instead, her relationships with students and families grew in surprising ways. As Charlotte began to feel more at ease with the curriculum and as she trusted herself to create and learn with her students, she relaxed. She shared bits of herself, like her own desire to learn to play the violin.

> I found a way to relax a little bit so that I could share a little bit about who I am and my personality, just in terms of sharing, being a person. [Colleagues] and I have talked about that too. That sharing yourself as a person, we've decided really creates a community in the classroom. If they know that I have things in my life that I struggle with, new things that I am learning, they see me.

Charlotte became vulnerable to her students; she trusted them. She felt "invested" in their lives. And, Charlotte found herself in some ways privy to the lives of people of color. She talked with joy about her relationship to one family whose three daughters she taught during her years at Mercer Elementary. She made visits to many families' homes, was invited to extracurricular activities by her students, and developed programs at school such as an annual author's fair to showcase student writing and attract families to the school.

DIFFICULT REFLECTIONS

Charlotte had been teaching for more than ten years in urban schools at the time of our interviews. In the retelling of her work life in urban schools, she named her fears. We discovered that some of her fears were race-based. However, Charlotte was deeply afraid of not being the kind of teacher she wanted to be. Also, it was clear that despite our years of friendship, she still had fears about talking about race. She was afraid to say the wrong thing.

But had no one asked, Charlotte would not have articulated her fears about becoming a white teacher. And, no one would have necessarily cared. Not speaking or remaining silent about race is commonplace. It is a "non-event" (Thandeka 1999, p. 10). White people are not supposed to talk about race, nor does it matter either way. Race is still thought of as an issue for people of color. And when white people have things to say and to try to figure out about race, they are afraid they will come across only as racist and an embodiment of privilege.

Amy Winans (2005) has pointed out "much scholarship still seems to essentialize whiteness, often presenting it as something that is interchange-able with white privilege" (p. 71). Winans argued the broad narratives that have been constructed about whiteness "efface the complexities of race in people's lived experiences and the role that emotions play in one's under-standing of those experiences" (p. 72). Charlotte struggled to find the right words to talk about her work experiences. Her "insights had outstripped her racial vocabulary" (Thandeka 1999, p. 12).

Attempts to map whiteness as a social construct have limited white peo-ple's ability to talk freely and to express emotion, causing further shame and less opportunity to take up more complex white identities. Critical scholar-ship has tended to "position whiteness as demonized, so that the only legiti-mate white stance is that of the race traitor" (Trainor 2002, p. 633).

There was another dimension to silence, shame, and fear about race. It is the inability of white people to talk to other white people about our experi-ences in nonwhite zones. In Charlotte's case, for example, she found herself remaining relatively silent in the face of racist talk in her personal social life for surprising reasons.

Charlotte reflected about how her racial self-concept had changed over the years. At first, she considered herself a bit of an "idealist." For a while she thought,

I can get the word out and inform and enlighten people about, not enlighten, but you know, open people's eyes to what is going on in our world right here. You know, how we should be, that shouldn't be allowed. It shouldn't be allowed that people don't have sheets on their bed and that if more people knew they wouldn't stand for it either.

Charlotte's sense of outrage and compassion, and her desire to make the world a better place, were shared by several of my participants. Charlotte found the conditions of the lives of her students unbearable. Her logic told her that if "everyone" knew, certainly something could be done.

Once, Charlotte had been on a mission trip to Haiti with an uncle who was a missionary. She volunteered to work in a school there for a week. She noticed how white people at home seemed to accept the idea of someone going to a "third world" country to help suffering children and families, and even to speak out against those conditions. Her feeling, after coming to know her own students well, was that "in our world right here" there were injustices. Early on, she thought it should be possible just to "open people's eyes" to these injustices and then other white people would become as outraged as she was.

She learned, however, that her family and friends were not as interested as she was in talking about her work, her students, and the conditions of their lives. It was hard to figure out what to do, because she did not want to become an outsider in her own white community of family and friends. She lost her certainty that "if more people knew they wouldn't stand for it either."

Charlotte felt that she was ineffective in moving other white people toward outrage or action with her knowledge of inequality and poverty. The import of Charlotte's experiences was that persuading someone of the fact of poverty or inequality was different from helping that person come to new explanations for inequality.

George Lipsitz (1995) described how, in the United States, it is usually assumed that individuals—through their talents and character—determine, for themselves, where they end up in our nation's social hierarchies. The fact or presence of inequality, then, under such an explanation, is not all that bothersome; is not, in fact, a problem. Charlotte's stories of poverty, then, did not respond to or counter what her white family and friends and colleagues took to be the causes of that poverty.

Charlotte told me that she responded to the challenges of talking about race, poverty, and her own teaching with other white people by not talking. This troubled me. I had been sure that she was pursuing an antiracist stance as a white teacher, that she wanted the best for her students. I explored this more with Charlotte. Why would she not speak out, defend misconceptions about her students, let stereotypes continue?

C: Before I would even enter a conversation like that, other than to say, if somebody is being really, you know, being really racist or being just really off-base and I know that that's not true. If I was hearing somebody saying "Well that's how everybody is in [this city]" I might say "Well not everybody." I would stand up that way. But I don't know. I think I've learned that unless somebody wants to see it, it's not a picture that I can paint for somebody just by telling them about it. Unless they really want to see it. And rather than get into an argument with somebody or, you know, just give them a forum to get loud about their points, it's just going to aggravate me. I just, I guess, I just pick and choose where I'm going to put that energy.

A: Uh huh.

C: Because if people don't want to see it they're not going to see it. So that makes me aware of my whiteness because there are a lot of white people that don't understand. They don't know. And there's . . . and it doesn't mean that they're bad and they don't know. But they just don't know, and—

A: Even if it's a conversation that is not about race explicitly, it is about race.

C: It is about race because they might be talking about [an area of this city] but in their mind they're picturing all black people. Or all minorities. Or all immigrants. Don't you think?

A: I agree with you.

C: Yeah. But that's just my . . . and I . . . yeah.

A: I just find it interesting that over time you've gotten more confident as a teacher but maybe less able to articulate your views to anyone.

C: Maybe less willing.

Charlotte's experiences working at Mercer Elementary, which has a nearly all African American student body, had given her insights into how her students lived, but at the same time it made her "less willing" to engage with other whites about her work.

She clearly had the privilege to choose not to speak. However, she used a strategy akin to that which the late activist and teacher Myles Horton used. He said, "I very seldom tell people what my position is on things when we're having discussions, because I don't think it's worth wasting the breath until they ask a question about it" (1990, p. 107).

Even when friends and family made stereotypical remarks, Charlotte did not think that, in comparison, she was a "good" white person. Further, she didn't see it as part of her job to reeducate others. She thought that by objecting to someone's stereotypical comments, she might be "giving them a forum to get loud about their points."

Nor did Charlotte want to become an outsider in her own white community of family and friends. Thandeka (1999) would argue that this fear of being excluded is central to the formation of white racial identities. For Charlotte, hearing stereotypical comments from others made her aware of her own white racial identity.

Charlotte figured, by hearing stereotypical comments again and again, that white people "don't understand" what she did. Most white people with whom she talked about Mercer thought that that area of the city was only about "the drugs and the guns and the gangs and the prostitutes and the people hanging out in the streets and crime and it's not safe and cars are being stolen and drive-by shootings."

> I think for people who haven't been in the home of somebody . . . who doesn't know them personally, sometimes the assessment of life in the Mercer neighborhood is [those people] are lazy, don't have a job, on welfare, not using birth control, you know all those negative things that aren't the complete picture.

When Charlotte said they just don't get "it," the "it" contains all of the tacit knowledge that she had gained over the years: from the workings of a bureaucratic urban district, to the standardized testing, to the poverty, to the racism, to the lives of the people whom she has come to respect and even love.

She said "it's not very fun to tell somebody's sob story to somebody that's not going to have any empathy. It's almost like exposing them . . . they'll still think it's just because somebody is lazy."

Before listening to Charlotte, my idea of being antiracist meant that white people must always speak out and speak up about racism. But Charlotte taught me that the very people whose lives we have become privy to as teachers deserve respect. And if that means staying quiet—if that means choosing not to engage—that could be a signal of respect and understanding. After all, why should we "tell somebody's sob story"?

Perhaps this is an overly sympathetic interpretation of Charlotte's actions and stories. Perhaps I should admonish her, myself, us, for not speaking out, acting boldly. Perhaps we must demand that family and friends listen to us and take our perspective as their own. How else will things change? How else will the lives of Charlotte's students and families, encased in violent institutions and a racist society, improve?

Charlotte knew that there were some sad and difficult issues in the lives of her students. And still:

> There are families sitting down to eat dinner at the table and kids playing in their backyards with their next-door neighbors. Just like what is going on in my neighborhood. Their parents are going to work every day and making very little money.

By being "less willing" to talk with others about Mercer, Charlotte was protecting her students and herself at the same time. She had come to see that not everybody shared her interest in students of color in urban schools.

> I think working in the city with a lot of different kids over several years exposes you to information . . . because you have a window into so many different people's lives. And that's being a teacher, I think. Every teacher has that window into so many people's lives.

Charlotte was trying to find, as Darrin says in the next chapter, "a sense of peace with being a member of this community." She entered naively into a nonwhite world to be an effective teacher of her students. Amidst the intensity of learning to teach and responding to her students' needs, she came to love her African American students.

> I don't know what else you want to hear about my story as a white teacher. I love teaching students of color and it's really hard for me to say why. The first time I was thinking about that I thought it's not because of their . . . color. It's because they're Jess and they're David and they're these kids. They're those people. But if I am honest with myself, it's not the same where I am now [at the white school]. I'm not as captured. I don't feel as captured emotionally— not in a bad way, but I don't feel the passion about the people, the kids. The only thing I've been able to come up with is we don't have the emotional level of interaction because the problems aren't there in the family. Also they don't need me in the same way. They don't need me emotionally really at all. Well that's not true. But they don't need me anywhere near the way I felt needed emotionally before. I guess any time you don't have that intense emotional interaction you don't feel as close to the people, because they're not sharing those experiences together. I guess that's it. So whatever the factors are that create that intense interaction I guess make me love it and miss it.

Charlotte embraced being a white teacher with black students. She became close to people of color for the first time in her life. None of her initial fears about student discipline or parental distrust stopped her from learning how to teach students through meaningful curriculum. She built loving relationships with many people of color. She was, in her words, "emotionally captured" and liked the way that she was "needed" by her students.

Working with white students, she said that "there just isn't the level of sharing whether it's a smile or laughter . . . if something is on their mind at home they can leave it at home and they can come to school and get through the day without me even needing to know anything ever." Charlotte liked connecting on a deep emotional level with people, all people. At Mercer that was one thing she liked, and she equated that with the African American students that she knew.

The white children in her new school were "flatter emotionally" and she did not feel as alive in her work life. Her teaching experiences after Mercer in a white community were less engaging to her emotionally and intellectually. She had lost a connection to students and their lives. She thought her white students needed her less and that challenged her purpose and identity as a teacher.

CONCLUSION

Charlotte no longer felt fully at home in a white community—something had been lost. Charlotte experienced a loss of voice in her own community. Her unwillingness to talk about her work in nonwhite zones alienated her from her family and later, in part, caused her to leave Mercer.

Perhaps this loss is unavoidable. And, of course, Charlotte's losses were not comparable to the losses, over centuries and across generations, of peoples of color. However, if Thandeka was at least partially right, then white people who become aware of being white at certain moments find themselves feeling not at home anywhere. They are no longer sure of their place in the white world when they cross into the nonwhite zone.

Charlotte and I struggled to talk about race—about our black students and ourselves as white teachers. I was surprised at the tensions we faced: how hard it was for her to find words; how hard it was for me to prod; how seriously we worked to talk things through. I had not planned to use Charlotte's interviews as part of my writing, but the lessons we learned were hard to ignore.

Many white people are ashamed to talk about race. Charlotte made this explicit during our interviews. But it was in those shame-filled spaces, in what was first unsaid and later, with care, uncovered, that we found the most significant insights. I suspect that Charlotte's story is like many white teacher stories. White teachers working with students of color often have intimate knowledge of students' lives. Unfortunately they do not have generative ways of talking about and making sense of what happens in those classroom spaces. Darrin, whose stories are in the next chapter, was one of those teachers too.

NOTES

1. This term comes from Thandeka (1999). She used nonwhite zones in reference to actual geographic locations and to "the subjective location within us where the resulting fear and submissive adjustments take up residence" (p. 21). Thus, the nonwhite zones are both outside and within us.

2. Othering connotes an emphasis on the (imagined/created) differences between black and white people and the tensions inherent in doing so.

Chapter Three

Darrin's Story: Authority and Control in the Classroom

Darrin invited me to interview him at his home on a tree-lined street of 1920s bungalows. He looked at me from his armchair with an easy smile and playful eyes. I noticed that his hands moved across his forehead as he talked. He said, "You just wanted me to talk about what it's like to be a white teacher in an urban district?" "Uh huh," I replied. He took a deep breath and deadpanned, "It was an adjustment." And went on to tell me his story, without pause, for nearly fifty minutes.

DARRIN'S WORK HISTORY

Darrin earned his license to teach English and theater for grades 7–12 while he worked as an educational assistant at a suburban middle school. After a student-teaching experience in the city that was "uncomfortable," Darrin was completely sure that he wanted to return to the suburbs as a teacher.

He reported, "I was fairly sure I was going to be hired there and work there. Forever." That work would have been predictable, even easy. And, as Darrin remarked with self-deprecating humor, "I'm usually . . . I'm all for the easy thing to do. I'm not a person that seeks out challenges or anything like that."

He had assumed that once he earned his license he would be hired at the same school, especially because he had "developed a theater program that was really vibrant." But much to his surprise:

> I actually didn't get hired. I didn't. I was shocked. There was a position that came available and the principal that I knew so well didn't hire me for it. So that was a real surprise. They wanted somebody who could coach hockey at the high school or something like that. So I ended up in [the city].

At first, Darrin took a long-term substitute position teaching theater at an urban performing arts elementary school. This meant he was taking over an elective class from a series of teachers who quit during the fall. He was a prep provider—a teacher who provides, in a sense, a planning break for the regular classroom teacher. He finished his student teaching in December and by January he had signed on to teach until June. Darrin took this job for purely pragmatic reasons.

> I'm not even licensed to teach elementary. I had been out of work for a long time and I had to have something. I had to do it. We were about to have a child. I needed a job. I needed to pay some bills.

Not only was Darrin not prepared to teach elementary-school students, he didn't want to teach in the city. As Darrin described it, he could not have been placed in a more challenging position: new teacher, unprepared to teach elementary education, and one of several teachers that year in the position.

But by far the most complicated piece of this work for Darrin had to do with race.

> Race was very, very apparent. That I could not reach or did not seem to have any kind of standing . . . or automatic . . . just because I was an adult which is what I was used to, you know, in the school environment you listen to the adults. The adults came with some authority and some respect and that was not there.

Darrin expected to be treated with respect. His experiences as a youngster taught him that children listen to adults. Growing up in the suburbs, he did not know anyone who challenged the teacher the way that he was challenged, and he attributed these behavioral differences to race. (The intermingling here of respect-the-adult and racial difference will be taken up and teased apart later. What was important here, from a researcher perspective, was that it was Darrin who brought these [related] issues to my attention.)

In this elementary school over 50 percent of its students were African American. Darrin believed the district called this school a "performing arts magnet" in order to attract white middle-class families. He thought that "performing arts magnet doesn't really describe the school" but acted as a label to help "balance" the school's racial and economic mix of children.

In the classroom Darrin had a difficult time connecting to the African American children. His curriculum included stories, games, and physical movement—all things he assumed young children of any color would enjoy. On the contrary:

> I started to become aware that African American girls especially and to some extent African American boys were especially difficult for me to reach. I had a lot of issues getting them to behave. Getting them to respond to my curriculum. They just simply weren't having it. And you know, I'm teaching theater, it's not like I'm teaching math or anything.

Darrin conceptualized a theater classroom as one where children would express themselves, move around, play games, and take up the responsibilities that come with being a student. Darrin struggled that winter. Reflecting on that first job, Darrin found it ironic that he simultaneously wanted the students to be orderly and participate.

> I was just pretty much helpless. I could not keep order in the classroom. I was so worried about keeping order in the classroom. I remember once I was dealing with first graders or kindergarteners or something like that and I was teaching them theater and I'm telling them a story and as I'm telling them the story they are getting up and they are acting out the story which is good you would think. But I was so concerned, I was saying, "Now sit down! Sit down! Everybody sit down and be quiet!" and afterward I was looking at my behavior and I was thinking, "My god, what is going on?" So it was a really hard job.

Darrin did not know how to keep order with students who seemed to have no respect for him. Student movement signified their presence and power in the classroom. He was scared and put off by his students' movement. He perceived it as a threat to his authority.

Just as it was important in the last chapter to explore Charlotte's beliefs about relationships with people in order to understand her better as a white teacher, it was important to understand Darrin's self-understanding about race to understand his experiences as a teacher. He had said that he thought he was a "liberal."

> I grew up in the suburbs and you know, I thought I was a liberal. I thought I was a . . . I didn't think of myself as a racist or anything like that. I didn't think of myself as having any real issues around race until I started working in [the city].

Darrin thought he was a liberal (and there is no reason to think he was not). He thought that, by being a liberal, he could not be a racist. He thought, by being a liberal, he did not have any issues to work out in relation to race. But he did.

David Theo Goldberg (1993) argued that liberal Western thought is actually quite wrapped up with racist thinking. It turns out that at the center of Western thought is not only the rational individual freeing itself from tradition and irrationality, but a *white* rational individual defined in opposition to an irrational, black other.

David Theo Goldberg (1993) explained:

> Liberal modernity denies its racialized history and the attendant histories of racist exclusions, hiding them behind some idealized, self-promoting, yet practically ineffectual, dismissal of *race* as a morally irrelevant category. By contrast, indeed, in resistance we might better confront just what it is about the notion of race that since the sixteenth century has . . . prompted thinkers silently to frame their conceptions of morality, polity, and legality in its terms. Liberal meliorism takes it that we have largely progressed beyond these racist social formations of the past. (p. 7)

Darrin, like many of us, was an heir to an idealized understanding of liberalism. Darrin, like many of us, wanted race to be "morally irrelevant." Darrin, like most of us, hoped that he and our society had "progressed beyond these racist social formations of the past." However, Darrin's self-understanding as a liberal fractured when he became a student teacher at an urban school.

It was the fall of 1996, the year of the O. J. Simpson murder trial. The nation was captivated by and talking about race. On the day that the verdict was read, he brought televisions into the classroom. Given that the story had dominated the news media and popular discussions for over a year, it seemed reasonable to bring current events into the classroom to use as a springboard for discussion. Darrin recalled his "life-changing" experience that day.

> When the verdict came out I was in a classroom, there was about fifty kids in this classroom and it was mixed races and we're all sitting there, many of us are standing, watching the verdict. When it happened and he was judged not guilty there was like this explosion in the room. And it was really apparent to me that there was a lot I did not understand about race. Every black kid in the room, every one of 'em was hollering and screaming and celebrating, you know, like the Super Bowl or the World Series or something. And every white kid just went, their heads just kind of "huh," and I was there too. I was sort of shocked. But more than what I was watching on television I was even more shocked by the reaction, by what was going on around me. And it was startling to me. And it was life-changing too.

Darrin said that before that "explosion in the room" he had believed he was a person who was "open, fair, not a racist." After the verdict was read, it became "really apparent to me that there was a lot I did not understand about race." He continued to explain his thinking.

I realized I don't understand the black experience. I have not a clue. Had not a clue. And I guess still, really in some ways don't have a clue of what it means to be African American in this country. And I think in that moment as I thought about it, and in that moment and later when I thought about the archetypes or the stereotypes or whatever—how many characters in stories and in television we've seen black men wrongly accused and strung up by white juries. As I thought about that, I put myself looking in it in that light and then seeing, seeing it from that light, trying to walk in, to be an African American and look at it in that perspective, and that, I mean, here was somebody that beat it that turned that archetype or turned that stereotype on its head.

All of this was a humbling experience for Darrin. If black and white kids could respond totally differently to an event, it did not mesh with his understanding of what it meant to a liberal. It became the impetus for him to continue his own racial understanding.

During the second interview, I asked Darrin to explain more about the O. J. verdict and what he called his "spiritual challenge." In the following exchange he responded to my question and elaborated on his thoughts.

A: Then you say something that I don't think I understand fully. Where you said, "but when that happened there" that was the O. J. thing, "there was something that clicked inside of me and I realized that there was this sort of profound spiritual challenge awaiting me" and I need to know more about that challenge.

D: I don't think I recognized it as a spiritual challenge at that moment. But there was something profound about that event. I think the dawning, when I realized that this work is of a spiritual nature to me. It is a . . . it is a . . . it's kind of a personal crusade. Because you know I've always said that I'm open and that I'm fair, that I'm not racist. That I don't believe in stereotypes. But the reality of this work and working with kids of color those fundamental notions about myself were being challenged and I realized—

A: So it was a spiritual challenge for yourself in—

D: Yes, yes—

A: In terms of what, in terms of trying to live out what you believed about yourself?

D: Right.

A: Ok. Right.

D: What I believed—

A: That you were open, liberal as you said, not racist—

D: I said liberal before? I didn't know if I used that word before. I said—[1]

A: Not racist.

D: Uh huh. Yeah. And I mean that's not only what I thought about myself but what I want to believe about myself. And that's what I aspire to. And that's never been challenged before.

Darrin worked to become the kind of person that he "aspires to" be. The O. J. verdict had shattered his racial self-knowledge. It was clear that he was not the kind of white person and teacher he had hoped he was.

For Darrin, the spiritual challenge was not a missionary one. Darrin explicitly stated that he did not intend to "save black children." The challenge, as he defined it, was to be "at peace" with the issue of being a white teacher working with children of color and being a member of the city's community.

DARRIN TEACHES THEATER

After two years teaching elementary school Darrin finally found a job teaching theater arts at an urban middle school. Darrin set the stage for the account of his work.

> It was a tough, tough school, a very tough school and middle school is a tough age. And again I walked in there and I had nothin'.[2] I had a stage, a huge, huge auditorium. It sat, I think it sat seven hundred to eight hundred people, and then a stage, and that's where I was supposed to teach theater. And of course they didn't bring me in because they wanted a theater program, they brought me in because they were so jam full and the only space that was available was the auditorium so "we could teach a class in here," "why don't we teach a theater class!" which was good, they didn't bring a math teacher in to teach. They had at least that much wherewithal. But I had nothin' when I first got there. Just nothin'. There was just me and an empty stage.

Given the rest of Darrin's stories, the repetition of "tough" can be read as a signal that his new students were students of color. He felt that middle-school students were "tough" as well.

While schools might not be set up well for students of any age, adolescents are particularly vulnerable in schools structured for obedience and control. From my own professional experiences I knew that middle-school students could be active, social, vocal, impulsive, and highly creative. In Darrin's case, he thought the administration made a good move by hiring an actual theater teacher—but by not supplying him with proper materials, he had "just nothin'" and felt bound to fail.

Still, Darrin had anticipated this moment for a long time. He was hired to teach in his licensure area with middle-school children. He was given an auditorium and not much else, but he was prepared with his curriculum— theater games, improvisational activities, and storytelling. The student population was a mix of mostly African American children, Hmong, Latino, and white. Once again Darrin was met with resistance.

> And the first day of school I said, "All right, come on in everybody, let's have a seat in a circle on the floor." "We ain't sittin' on the floor." I mean right, the very first thing I said. "No we're not doing that." "I ain't doin' that." "I ain't sittin' on the floor." And, oh man, that's, it was pretty much like that for the first semester. In fact it got worse. It was just . . . it was very difficult. These kids had no clue, no understanding of what I was trying to do. They didn't have any sense of what the arts were, of what theater was, of my discipline.

Darrin told me that he "suffered." The first day was quite a shock; he thought he was prepared and ready to teach. Yet from the first moment the students were rejecting him and his program. It could have been that the students were simply challenging authority as middle-school kids sometimes do. Or, perhaps they were just rejecting the adult in the room. But, for Darrin, this was about race.

During this first month teaching drama Darrin became seriously ill. He knew that the timing was "unfortunate" and when he returned a few weeks later he considered quitting. Teaching was chaotic and overwhelming. It was in some ways similar to his first experience teaching elementary school. He was met time and again with resistance and could not manage the students. And he looked inward, feeling like a failure.

> There were children . . . there were children all over the auditorium. It was a huge space. And as soon as they came in the door instead of sitting in a circle on the stage they would see this vast enormous space and they would just charge into it, run into it screaming and hiding under the stage. And I mean it was a just a nightmare, a nightmare. And I had no standing . . . I thought I understood the middle-school psyche because I had worked for several years with middle-schoolers in [the suburban school]. It was an enormous blow to me personally. I thought, "I just don't understand the first thing about educating these children. I have no idea what I am doing." So, it was frightening.

Darrin had reached a crossroads. He wanted to share his love of the theater arts with students but his inability to create a space that was conducive to students taking both the pleasure and responsibilities that come with theater was unbearable. He thought he understood middle-school students because he had done similar work in the suburbs. The "nightmare," then, was in teaching "these children": children of color. Darrin began to understand that his students

> had no clue of what I was trying to teach them. And in fact I had given up trying to teach them and I was just trying to entertain them, get them quiet. You know these were children who didn't really even want to hear my stories. And I have some good stories. I mean it was really an ego-deflating experience.

When Darrin couldn't maintain control—teach the way he desired—it was a blow to his ego. Who am I if I can't even tell stories that entertain? If that was who Darrin thought he was—an engaging and entertaining storyteller—then who was he going to be in relationship to his students, who he really did not have "a clue" about? His experiences caused crisis. Darrin was losing any sense of agency or power, and with it, his sense of self. The way that Darrin described it, he was near "rock bottom" personally.

> I remember just being exhausted, day in and day out, just totally exhausted. I'm not a drinking man anymore. I used to be. I stopped using drugs and chemicals a long time ago. I think I would have died, I think I just would have [had I not stopped using]. I think it was the kind of life that I just would have spent the entire . . . I would have spent large amounts of time in a bar afterward just trying to relax and unwind. I didn't have that option so I think I did a lot of sleeping and I just maybe watched a lot of TV. And I don't know how I coped.

Amazingly, Darrin did not quit. Instead, he got serious about making it work for himself and his students. He brought in two friends from the community, a white psychologist and an African American theater friend, who observed his classes and began to coach him. Darrin began to take charge of his students through developing curriculum to build community in the classroom founded upon principles of nonviolence.

> The three of us started to work up a plan about how to take back control of the classroom and how to start teaching theater. And we came up with this nonviolent curriculum, elements of which I still use.

His call for help and support from outside the school, and of note, from a knowledgeable member of the African American community, proved to be the right step for Darrin.

In his second year at the middle school he applied for grants. With that seed money and the support of his professional friends, he developed a theater program that slowly gained momentum.

I started to build the kind of theater program, well actually, I started building a totally different kind of theater program than I had built in [the suburban school]. Instead of being all after school this was all right during school. And instead of being most filled with mostly white girls and you know this sort of "aren't we pretty" theater, this was filled up with a lot of African American boys who needed the outlet, who needed the rap, needed to dance, needed the physicality. [pause] There was some successes there.

Theater, for his students, became a place for them to express themselves, during school, in intellectual, physical, and emotional ways. They moved, they improvised, and they performed in ways that were teacher-approved.

Darrin created a rudimentary set of binaries for himself using his suburban and urban teaching experiences. There were contrasts between white/ black, desire/need, pretty/physical. The contrasts were sharp, perhaps overdrawn, and even a touch stereotypical. Darrin's perceptions were valuable nonetheless. Darrin, the white teacher working with students of color, was beginning to create curriculum that matched his students' needs. The theater classroom was becoming more about them than him.

As Darrin told stories that served to orient him in a "moral space" (Taylor cited in Knowles [2003], p. 33), he situated himself as both making progress in his teaching *and* struggling along with students whom he could not reach. Darrin was feeling a bit more hopeful about his ability to get his theater program off the ground because of the support of his grants, his colleagues outside the school, and a "large amount of kids that were with me and wanting to learn." Simultaneously he found himself

way too distracted . . . and paying too much attention to the kids that, well, they were unteachable, some of them. I mean I hate to say it but at that point in time, for that minute, for me where I was at, they were unteachable. I didn't have what it took to teach them.

Darrin developed at least two conceptions of himself as a theater teacher in relation to his students. He found that there were students who engaged, complied, and perhaps enjoyed his class. He was no longer frightened of the majority of the students who he has said were "with him." They were the students he could reach.

But there were the students who were "unteachable," a surprisingly honest word choice especially considering the current educational discourse that "all children can learn" and "no child left behind." Darrin knew, however, that students who he considered unteachable were so, at least in part, because of his *own* inadequacies. He did not "have what it took to teach them." It was a painful, honest admission. In simple terms, Darrin was both a success and a failure.

One student who challenged Darrin immensely was Antonio, an outstanding theater student who, for myriad reasons, did not behave consistently well in the classroom. Darrin initially effused both praise and worry about Antonio and his brother.

> The two of them made brilliant theater together. I mean they were incredible. They had incredible improvisational skills, incredible verbal skills. And they were funny and they had, in some ways, they had a lot going for them. They didn't have the right parents. And these two guys, they kept me up at night because they were such brilliant theater students and yet they were failing my class because they couldn't do . . . the regular things didn't apply to them . . . And they just kept me up at night.

After Darrin's introduction of the brothers, he told two utterly captivating stories about Antonio. Both stories begged exploration and interpretation of ways in which the teacher and the student or the white man and black adolescent struggle for power, disrupt school norms, and, in doing so, find fleeting moments of control. The first story I call "Fire and Ice," and the second, "The Kiss."

Fire and Ice

Darrin used some of his grant money to make masks with students, an activity designed to teach about character in theater. One day, in the midst of mask making, he and the students hurried outside in response to a fire drill.

> And I remember working on the mask with Antonio and there was a fire drill. We went outside. There was snow. And Antonio started throwing ice chunks at some of his classmates and there was this snowball fight and stuff like that and I tried to stop it. And Antonio was just not hearing me. It was like I was invisible.

So there they were, in the midst of a snowball fight while Darrin was supposed to demonstrate that he could keep his students in a line and quiet—the proper procedure for a fire drill. He was ignored by Antonio. Antonio seemed to neither hear nor see Darrin. He continued the story.

> I was like right next to him and I was trying to tell him to settle down and he was just wild, he was just crazy. And I finally, I grabbed him. Grabbed his shirt actually. And he immediately sort of tore himself away and his shirt ripped. And ah, and that became this . . . this . . . this incident.

"This incident" spiraled out of control in several ways. First, Antonio told his father that his theater teacher tore his shirt. Then, during a phone conversation, Antonio's father called him a "motherfucking faggot and all sorts of stuff." Darrin felt that the father was "just totally threatening, totally abusive." Darrin was frightened of Antonio's father and angry with the school principal.

In Darrin's mind he was "trying to do right" by Antonio in trying to stop him from throwing ice chunks at his peers, but in the wake of ripping his shirt "all that was lost." Darrin recalled angrily that the principal did not support his version of the story. He thought he was trying to stop a fight when a boy's shirt ripped. But the principal did not stand with him.

> [The principal] didn't back me at all. It just became this . . . uh . . . and then [Antonio's] father called me and threatened my life . . . Called me a motherfucking faggot and all sorts of stuff. Just totally threatening, totally abusive. And then he called the principal and he did a totally different act. Cause the principal said "well he's making sense to me, he's sounding . . . going to call a lawyer" and stuff like that and I was really . . . I was angry and I was frightened.

Was the phrase "motherfucking faggot" just spontaneous profanity, or did Antonio's dad use it purposefully to suggest that Darrin was gay? Was Antonio feeling threatened because he liked theater? Was it was perceived by his father as an effeminate thing to do? (These questions will return in the next story "The Kiss," which centered on issues of heternormativity and control.)

In either case, Darrin was angry and frightened. After the "incident" in the snow, Darrin began to second-guess himself. Between what he remembered and the negative responses of Antonio, his parents, and the principal, Darrin said:

> I honestly couldn't tell. It's like most racial violence—you don't really know where the truth is. Where the truth was. I can't remember exactly how his shirt ripped. I don't know. I began to question what the truth was. I do know that I was trying to do right by him. But that was lost.

The truth certainly was elusive. Was Darrin doing something more aggressive than he was willing to remember or admit? Antonio had been a difficult student all along. Was Darrin pushed too far?

Darrin felt isolated and alone at school. He knew that unless there was a fight among students, teachers did not have the support of the administration. In this case, not only did the principal not back him, he even backed off from finding out what may have happened when he heard that Antonio's father was thinking of bringing a lawyer into it.

With the benefit of time and reflection, Darrin said "certainly, my laying hands on a kid was violent or even a kid's clothing, was in his eyes violent. It was an act of aggression." Antonio's parents undoubtedly "saw this big white teacher picking on their thirteen-year-old son."

This was an event which began playfully. Antonio was playing with snow. It was only when he began to throw ice chunks at others and began to taunt them that the event turned from play to violence. This quick shift took Darrin by surprise.

> They were being kids. It was a snowball fight and it was a play thing. But it was fairly violent. And certainly my laying hands on a kid was violent or even a kid's clothing was in his eyes violent. That, I think, is what I came to realize. I don't think at the time I thought I was being violent. But when you look at the results and then you flip it around and look at how that family interpreted it. Um, it was an act of aggression against their child. That's what they saw, you know.

Over time, Darrin began to interpret this not only as a teacher/student incident, but also a racially loaded one, as suggested by the outraged response by Antonio's father. And, despite his anger and fear toward Antonio's parents, he was able to understand their anger about what happened to their son.

Amidst these competing and shifting interpretations of the event, I want to turn now to look at the ways in which Darrin positioned Antonio. Darrin was trying to stop the fight, get control of the situation, and get control of Antonio's body. Darrin thought Antonio was "wild, he was just crazy."

As I imagine the two of them in the snow during a fire drill, I cannot help but hear echoes from our society's awful racist past. My mind drifts away from the specific image of Darrin and Antonio in the snow. The school becomes a plantation. I see a slave owner. I see a slave. I see the slave owner laying his hands on a slave. It is violent. It is all violent.

Darrin's story rumbled with the idea that those with power (whites) ought to control the wild, unfettered beasts who are only partly human (nonwhites). But this story was not just about white supremacy and racial oppression; it was also about the ways Western thought views childhood.

According to Nancy Lesko (1996), imperial discourse imagined and justified more than just white male supremacy. There were also implications for views on the development of the child into a proper adult. Adolescence was "deemed the dividing line between rational, autonomous, moral white bourgeois men and emotional, conforming, sentimental, or mythical Others, namely primitives, animals, and children" (1996, p. 460).

Further, and drawing on Stuart Hall's work, Lesko wrote:

> The youth-as-primitive analogy constructs adolescents in the same terms that subject peoples were defined: irrational, conforming, lazy, emotional beings who were totally other from Euro American adult men. (p. 461)

On one level, Antonio was just a kid throwing ice and snow during a fire drill, and Darrin was just a teacher trying to stop him. Read through the lens of colonialism (or the underbelly of Western liberal thought [Goldberg 1993]), Darrin was white and had the burden to dominate the black other, Antonio, for his own good. Darrin was the adult and had the responsibility to control the primitive-adolescent, Antonio. Darrin and Antonio took their parts in an old but modern tale, a struggle among the privileged and the discounted for control, for authority, and for meaning.

The Kiss

After the snowball fight Antonio was transferred out of Darrin's theater class. But, as things go in schools, two years later Antonio was back in his class as an eighth-grader. "There were times when he was just uncontrollable," Darrin said.

It was during one of those times that Darrin did something that, now, in our interview, he hesitated to say.

D: And this is not something I am proud of at all but it goes, it shows kind of what I was reduced to [nervous laughter], you know, working with these kids. There was a day when Antonio, he was just kind of, he was prancing around behind me, he was calling, you know, basically he was mimicking me in the theater class. You know, just kind of playing around and getting kids to laugh and he was sissifying me. He was acting really gay and stuff like that. And I noticed it. And I just kind of ignored it and kept on going. And at one point I just turned around and I went [makes a kissing noise] like that to him.

A: OH!

D: And ah, it ah, he went absolutely ballistic. It scared the bejeezus out of him. He just went ballistic. And you know, um and I, I suddenly realized "Oh my god, I got you!" [laughter] and I didn't stop. I wouldn't stop, you know, I just kept on doing it and stuff and he just went ballistic. He totally, he was going totally crazy and I called the administration they came in and they saw this child going out of his mind and they carted him off.

There were myriad, complicated issues presented in this narrative, which was, at the very least, a racial text and a gendered text.

There was Antonio on stage, in a theater class. He was performing. He was effective, too. Darrin called him "brilliant." So, he pranced and he "sissified" Darrin. In doing so he got the attention of his classmates and his teacher. He was doing something out of bounds for a student (but perhaps not out of bounds for a theater student).

Nevertheless, he was making fun of the teacher. He was in control, he had the audience laughing, and he was putting his teacher down. From the kind of theater atmosphere Darrin has described, one wonders if they both might have laughed along with the audience.

Thinking back to the snowball incident that occurred two years prior, perhaps there was something extra-charged for Darrin in the "sissifying" part. Remember Antonio's father had called Darrin a "motherfucking faggot"—perhaps there were rumors circulating that Darrin was gay and/or maybe Antonio had harbored ill will toward this teacher who had ripped his shirt. Was this a way for Antonio to reject Darrin as a human being?

Darrin took up control of the script in the drama that Antonio began two years earlier with the snowball incident. He turned around and (gleefully?!) blew an air kiss to Antonio, thereby turning the tables on his misbehaving student. Until now Antonio had been suggesting that Darrin was gay and that he, Antonio, was not. Now, there was the possibility that Antonio was gay, that he had beckoned the kiss from Darrin and that the prancing around had been not mimicry of the teacher, but his own walk/dance/prance. This was most certainly not what Antonio had imagined when he started mocking his teacher.

At this moment in the first interview, I ad-libbed an unwelcome editorial into the script with a loud "OH." I had not for a moment thought that Darrin would enter into Antonio's drama in that way. In the second interview, Darrin commented on my reaction: "It's offensive to you." I couldn't disagree. He continued:

> Yeah, you know it was just . . . you know I mean, oh god, it was ah, working at that place was really . . . really . . . I was really alone. And in when I get alone and I don't know how it is for other people, but when I get alone I lose touch with who, with what I am, and I start to stray from my own values.

The blowing of the kiss made Antonio angry and scared—just how Darrin felt when Antonio's father called him after the shirt tore and Darrin realized that the principal would not back him.

Darrin did something unexpected and garnered some power back; he humiliated Antonio in front of his peers. Antonio didn't realize the potential consequences of his mockery of his teacher and that Darrin would act in ways that were outside of the normally sanctioned role of a teacher. Maybe Antonio behaved that way because he felt that there wouldn't be any consequences that he cared about, in other words, being kicked out of class, suspended—those things didn't matter. But being humiliated, being considered as possibly gay—of course that mattered.

And Darrin gained pleasure and control. He laughed. He realized his out-of-bounds response was exactly the thing that would give him the upper hand. His improvised kiss in the air became a classroom-management tool and he continued to use it to control Antonio. Like the play snowball fight turned violent, the playful, teasing, sissifying drama turned into yet another violent, serious moment when the teacher (re)asserted control over the student.

That Darrin felt Antonio was "going totally crazy" was important too. After all, this was a student who in a sense drove Darrin crazy—he made brilliant theater *and* didn't follow the rules. Darrin was up at night trying to figure out what to do with him, he was in one sense "crazy" with concern, worry, and even disdain about this student. Antonio drove Darrin crazy.

Darrin reasserted his institutional authority when he called for help and locked Antonio out of his classroom. And this time he seemed to have the school on his side. When the administration "came in and saw this child going out of his mind, they carted him off." Once Antonio was gone, Darrin locked himself and his students in the classroom.

> I did something I've never done before. I locked the doors. I remember, I locked the doors and I didn't answer the phone as soon as I got him out. And I just went ahead teaching. I remember we were doing something fairly quiet and it was a candlelight activity, some kind of storytelling, or something like that, so I was really glad to get rid of him. I was really glad to get rid of him.

Darrin's initial descriptions of Antonio and his brother were positive images—two talented, brilliant, incredible theater kids. Darrin mentioned that their parents weren't the "right ones," which I interpreted as Darrin's way of saying the boys were not well supported at home, not "parented" in the way that he might parent his own children. Perhaps he meant if they had the right parents they would be able to follow the rules and still make brilliant theater together. But did they make such brilliant theater because they did not follow the rules?

These two brothers kept Darrin up at night because they were brilliant and failing his class. He had rules, a system—students must do the written work, show up on time, attend class, and listen to instructions.

These two brothers refused to play by Darrin's rules. Darrin, in the end, asserted control by breaking his own rules. Darrin ended this story by telling what happened later in the day.

> They didn't suspend him cause I saw him in the hall later on and now he was all fronting, and he's telling everybody "this guy is gay, this guy is gay" and I just did it [the air kiss] again and it was childish. Actually, it was really childish but it was the first time that I felt like I had any kind of leverage with this child, that I could control his behavior. And all I had to do was purse my lips and blow him a kiss. So the upshot, the good thing, was that the administration took the easy way out. And they just took him out of my class. And so I got distracted with Antonio. That's a sad, sad story.

Darrin was glad that Antonio was gone from his class. His story was accepted and Antonio was removed (permanently) from his class. When he looks back his conclusion was that it was "a sad, sad story."

CONCLUSION

In both "Fire and Ice" and "The Kiss," Darrin and Antonio were entangled in events that began as play and quickly shifted into scenes of violence and humiliation. Years later, Darrin believed that he would do "things differently" with a similar type of student.

> If I had another Antonio I would have to . . . if I recognized myself in a situation again . . . if there was another kid who exhibited the same kind of brilliance and the same kind of outlandishness and out-of-bounds behavior . . . I would have to do things differently. I would have to avoid getting into any kind of power struggle with him. It is such a messed-up situation.

Darrin theorized part of what caused the "power struggle" with Antonio was his own descent into adolescent-like behavior. Sometimes it is "okay and good" to realize we are not always capable of being in control, he said, because the reality is:

> I'm expected to always be in control. And I should always be in control and, certainly, I should be in control of my emotions and what I say to other children. But the reality is that I'm going to make mistakes. And I don't think I'm going to go in as deep to that dark adolescent rage as I used to.

Darrin's language here was stunning. He shifted from describing his relationship to Antonio to describing the relationship between different parts of himself. In order to remain in control, he said that he would not go "in as deep to that dark adolescent rage."

Dark adolescent rage—in this phase, Darrin linked, as Lesko (1996) did, the discourses of adolescence and colonialism. He also provided a striking example of what Fiedler (1964) argued has happened throughout American history: that white people (especially white males) have used people of color to work through and describe unacceptable or troublesome parts of themselves.[3]

In addition, Darrin's words exposed the chimera of colonial ideology. The story was supposed to go this way: he was an adult and he was white, therefore *he was in control*. But the reality was that he was not in control. Darrin knew this. He said that "if we have any soul at all we have to connect with that part of ourselves occasionally."

And Antonio, on some level, knew that Darrin was not in complete control because he was able to take up a relationship with his theater teacher that exposed more complicated ways of being a black adolescent. A mythical story would have us believe that the binaries white/black and adult/adolescent are static. While I am not suggesting that Antonio was successful in completely flipping the story on its head, the above event was a disruption in the usual script—that fleeting moment when power shifted.

As Lesko (1996) explained:

> Most often when conflict between adolescents and adults is described, teenagers are defined as rebellious, that the source of the conflict is within them. The concrete interactions of rebellious youth with adults are seldom made visible, so that the simple, unitary description of teenagers as rebellious stands. In this way the discourse on adolescents tends to produce a fixed opposition between adults and youth, approaching the Manichean opposition of the colonizer and the colonized. (p. 469)

One risk in flipping the script around was that, while it opens possibilities for new roles and relationships, it can also put people in dangerous, scary places.

Darrin said he felt alone and out of touch with his values. When he tried to stop Antonio from throwing ice he felt "invisible." Perhaps his identity as a liberal, white, male, heterosexual teacher was compromised—that it was not sane for him to take up and try on identities that felt out of control.

Surely Antonio felt alone on that stage being positioned as a gay black adolescent. He was further pushed to the margins of school. The descent for both into "unfettered" and free movement, in a struggle for control on the stage, also became a struggle to stay whole, to stay connected.

Darrin told these two provocative stories of his work life as a white teacher because they were important to him and he knew that his struggle for control was worth exploring. He struggled to control the learning environment and the students' habits and actions in the classroom. He struggled to keep thinking of himself as an effective teacher, and ultimately he struggled to understand and control who he was—both who he wanted to be and who he was being, moment to moment. The spiritual journey for Darrin was about being true to his values. The stories were about the limits of those liberal values.

NOTES

1. A rechecking of the transcript confirmed that Darrin did specifically use the word "liberal."

2. Darrin uses "nothin'" repeatedly for emphasis about his working conditions. I purposely decided to keep "nothin'" as I heard it repeatedly on the tape (as well as in person during the interview). I believe he wanted me to hear it that way and he used it for dramatic effect.

3. Fiedler, writing in 1964, put it this way: "Ask any American for his attitude toward Indian and Negro, and you will discover his attitude toward his own impulsive life; or conversely, find how any American deals with his own basic drives, and you can guess his attitudes toward our colored minorities" (p. 125).

Chapter Four

Desire, Care, and (Mis)Reading Whiteness

Teachers work and live within institutions and structures that are not made and remade in the best interest of everyone. Conscious efforts toward reshaping and remaking education for children of color is a racial project of immense proportions.

Teachers have limited agency to make radical, systemic changes to curriculum and to the way schools are structured. Historian and curriculum theorist Herbert M. Kliebard (1995, 2002) reminded us that education elites and policy makers have long struggled over the goals, methods, and curricula of public education, usually with little reference to the expertise and desires of teachers (and community members).

Furthermore, as the research of William H. Watkins (2001) has made clear, the schools developed for blacks after the Civil War and on into the twentieth century were explicitly set up, not for social or individual advancement, but to maintain the prevailing social order and quell widespread concerns about the "Negro problem" (for further reading c.f. Kliebard [2002]; DuBois [1903/1997]; Winfield [2007]).

For example, one white "architect" of black education was General Samuel Chapman Armstrong, the founder of the Hampton Institute in Virginia. Modeled on colonial ideology, the Hampton Institute "would be a manual labor school . . . it would provide training in character building, morality, and religion to 'civilize' the 'childlike' and 'impetuous' Negro" (Watkins 2001, p. 48).

For Watkins, Armstrong was trying to prove "to the world" that:

His Blacks could look and act respectable by White standards. They were quiescent and conforming. They demonstrated a level of intelligence that justified Hampton's attracting additional funding. They could not appear uppity or threatening to the social order of their own subservient position in the South . . . he understood the political economy of peonage and where Blacks 'fit.' They would always be semicitizens with semifreedom. (pp. 51–53)

It follows, rightfully so, that there is great suspicion today among people of color and critical theorists about the future of schools in the United States and about the capacity of white people to teach black children well. Can white teachers, given this history and these institutions, teach students of color in ways that can ensure their academic and social success?[1]

In this chapter I examine the stories of three teachers, Paul, Frida, and Margaret. My claim is not (necessarily) that they are successful teachers of students of color—I do not have the sort of evidence to make such a claim. But important things were happening in their work with students, and their practices and experiences led them to important understandings of themselves as white teachers of students of color.

But these understandings were not simple or straightforward. Because Paul, Frida, and Margaret were working in an educational system set up, not for liberation (Freire 1973), but for submission and control, because they carry with them meanings and feelings influenced by a white supremacist society (including their families), there was much to sort out about themselves and their work. The teachers read or interpreted themselves as white teachers and as a white people against a backdrop of history, popular culture, and educational research. I develop three interrelated themes in relation to these teachers and their experiences: white teachers' desires; the complexities of caring in schools; and the difficulties we experience when we try to interpret white teachers' words, stories, and desires.

This chapter extends ideas from the previous chapters. Charlotte's stories illustrated the complexity of talking about race and making sense out of caring for students and their families. Darrin's stories illustrated the harm and violence that occurred amidst his desire to teach well.

My worry here is basic: I worry about simple categorizations of white people: simple readings, misunderstandings. Simple readings of people of color have contributed to horrific violence. These readings have not worked for people of color and they never will. Because of white privilege, however, a misreading of white people does not have the same horrific consequences. But if we want to make sense of teaching, of white teachers working with students of color, we must resist simplification.

First, I share a story from my own life—a reading (or misreading) of what I thought it meant to be a good white activist. I use this example to begin an exploration in this chapter of how white teachers (and often the researchers who study them) misread who they are as racial actors in schools.

CONFESSIONS OF A QUIET ACTIVIST

I've been thinking a lot about the day I sat in a library, as a teenager, reading Martin Luther King's famous speech. How moved I was. His speech mixed with other stories in my mind, to create coherence about the way to fight against racism and sexism.

I was born in 1968, although when I was a young person, I wished I would have been born earlier. Then I could have marched at Selma, protested at Kent State, registered voters in Mississippi, worn my hair long, burned my bra, stopped shaving my armpits, shouted, waved my fists, attended radical poetry readings, smoked marijuana, and discussed loudly the state of the world with other like-minded youth.

I know now that this was a white middle-class girl's dream—that more often females in the 1960s were working, attending school, and tending to babies. (My own mother couldn't or wouldn't attend the now infamous protests at the Democratic National Convention in Chicago. She reminded me that I was only twenty-seven days old. How on earth would she, could she, have gone?).

The images I constructed as a teenager missed many of the behind-the-scenes complications associated with any social movement. Later, I would learn that the civil rights movement was not a cohesive group of like-minded people talking about peace. There was violence. People died (would I go that far?). The women's movement, I discovered, was really a *white* women's movement.

All of it was much more complicated than I had once believed. But at that time, the more I read about the civil rights movement, the more I yearned to be a part of something so radical, so revolutionary, so catastrophic. And that was *the way to be an activist*. My image of a good white activist remained static for many years: it takes a lifetime to unlearn the things we learn as children. And, it is in the unlearning that we can imagine more complicated ways of living, of acting, of being someone who can make change in our own complicated ways.

What happened to that image when I began my work as a teacher in urban schools? The students were usually children of color who lived in poverty. I saw that there was a fight to fight, wrongs to be righted, a new generation suffering the effects of poverty, racism, sexism, every -ism in the book. But there were no movements for me to join. No marching for me to do. Just close my door and teach. *It was so quiet*. No one was listening, not even people I worked with. No one was mad like me.

And I became more and more frustrated by the solitary revolution. It was just inside me and I was alone, except that I was with my students. I tried to teach them to be revolutionary. We did projects about their health, about racism, about the Holocaust, violence, AIDS, and other tragedies that we found compelling. The students were with me. We read and wrote and talked about what we called "important issues." We learned, they learned. But still, nothing happened. Nothing that I considered revolutionary.

I share these thoughts and images in order to frame this discussion in terms of the ways in which this research has challenged me to reconsider my own previous beliefs about what it would look and feel like to be white, good, and revolutionary, or said another way, the right way to be white. I have struggled to find a way to write about these feelings and impulses without sounding sappy or sentimental. I am aware, as David Hansen (1995) wrote, "To romanticize and sentimentalize teaching is analytically sterile. It inflicts on teaching and teachers the same disservice as accounts that reduce the practice to a by-the-numbers recipe" (p. 114).

Therefore, as I analyzed the transcripts and read in these teachers' stories a sense of care toward the students, a sense of commitment toward their learning, toward the community, and toward being a good teacher, I also noticed how they read and misread their own journeys as white teachers and as white people within a multiplicity of racial contexts.

In this spirit, what follows is a series of portraits of three participants. Like me and Charlotte, they might be considered "quiet activists." By not marching loudly against the inequities in the system, these white teachers would not usually be seen as having a role in the revolution. Their work is quiet. It is not heard, seen, valued—for if it were there would be more spaces and places in the educational system for kids and teachers to develop meaningful, lasting, loving relationships involving learning, teaching, and passions. This ambivalence toward white urban teachers continues to trouble researchers and teachers alike. How are we supposed to be? How *are* we?

PAUL

Paul told his story about his work as a white teacher in a straightforward way. He respected his students' experiences and the ways that their parents worked to support them. As caring as Paul was, he did not mince words when he described how "crazy" urban teaching could be.

I worked in really sort of a hard-core school in [this city]. It was just crazy. But I always just enjoyed the kids. Sometimes their behaviors drove me nuts, what they did drove me nuts sometimes. But there was always this underlying . . . I could still see the kid inside it all. It's like, you're a fifth grader, you're obnoxious most of the time, you've got all these issues but you're still . . . every once in a while, there's this glimpse of this kid who wants to be a kid, wants to do the best they can do. But they're just in a place where it's just so hard to focus on school. I think they need someone who can see that in them because I think a lot of adults don't see that; they think oh, "it's a problem, they are troublemakers." I never really saw them that way.

A "hard-core" school was one that might conjure up notions of a stereotypical urban school inasmuch as Paul mentioned the students' problem behavior (not unlike Darrin's use of the word "tough"). Undoubtedly some students were not behaving in ways he expected students to behave. Still, Paul "could still see the kid inside it all."

Paul's desire and capacity to see beyond student misbehavior (perhaps unlike Darrin) did not create a crisis of authority. In fact, he distinguished himself from other adults whom he heard say that a particular student was a "problem" or a "troublemaker." Pathologizing-the-child discourse was available, certainly—as Paul pointed out. But for Paul, it was a discourse actively rejected.

He was able to recognize that the kids "want to do the best they can do," but there were myriad reasons why it was hard: the school environment, the developmental stage of the child, the complexities of peer social relationships, or the particular mood of the day.

Paul's recognition of some of the inherent challenges for students in his "hard-core" school were not excuses or evidence that he felt sorry for them and would have been a less-demanding teacher. Instead, Paul understood the various influences and challenges faced by the students with whom he worked.

Paul's story of his work as a white teacher in urban schools working with students of color came across as remarkably compassionate. How did he get this way?

In our second interview Paul tried to explain what in his early life experiences had shaped his perspectives. "I've learned to try to see things the ways that other people would see them, but I don't know what is so appealing about that," he said. Paul, without understanding why, took up an empathetic perspective.

Paul's interpretation of his role as a teacher came, in part, from his earlier experiences as a social worker. He worked for a nonprofit organization that provided various services for families, including a daycare for small children and adult employment training. He said that he felt a kinship with his co-workers. It was easy for him to work with like-minded people.

> I felt immediately at home with the staff, the sort of issues that they were
> concerned about were the same things I was concerned about. They sort of
> understood why these kids were like they were. Kids who were struggling in
> school wasn't because they didn't have parents who care, it wasn't because
> they hadn't been trying, it was because you know, school for one reason or
> another isn't working out whether it's home or the way stuff that's presented
> in school hasn't interested them, their perspective, or how they've grown up.

There is certainly research in teacher education that makes it seem as if
saying that "we care" is a bad thing. Marx (2001) discussed preservice white
teachers' talk. She interpreted their discussions about their role as tutors to
students of color as "embedded in a 'caring and sharing' storyline" in which
they tried to be "warm, loving, friendly, and personable"—so that the kids
could have someone who cared about them, "even for a few months" (p.
124). Marx was troubled that somehow the act of tutoring represented a way
of bestowing upon or maintaining distance and superiority to the children.
Marx's work demonstrated the problematic assumptions that white tutors had
in relation to their students, and in doing so highlighted a bind we white
researchers and teachers find ourselves in.

Most people would agree that teachers should care about their students;
but in what ways should they care? How should they demonstrate that care?
And, most importantly, within a racially constructed discourse, how are
white teachers positioned when they admit to and talk about caring about
their students?

Paul cared for students in a way that reflected a reading of connections
between race, poverty and a system that impacts the individual lives within
it. His knowledge did not separate him from Marx's research participants
who entertained racist beliefs, for Paul readily discussed the racism within
himself.

> I take the bus sometimes to work and if all of a sudden there's a group of black
> teenage boys on the bus, you start thinking, you know, I don't know, there's
> thoughts that come into your head like oh, you know, what are they going to
> do? What kind of trouble are they going to cause? Which, I've really tried to
> get over that, like thinking, they're just kids they could just be trying to get
> from one place to another like everybody else on this bus. So those thoughts
> come into your head.

Paul acknowledged systemic effects on people. He did workshops and reading about working with urban students, although it was the home visits he
made as a social worker that left the biggest impression on him. Never
having experienced poverty first hand, Paul's work brought him in close
contact with families who lived in poverty.

> I think it just opened my eyes to how other people live. Like poverty. What it was. It is not something these people are choosing to do by any means. It's not something they want for their kids. I mean they all want . . . there's this stereotype of like, you know, you don't value education, you don't do anything for your kids, your kids are struggling in school and it's all your fault. I was just like, man, you are doing everything you can just to get food on the table. To try to be a mom . . . a lot of them were single moms. So it just sort of opened my eyes to that whole world.

Paul saw beyond the popular stereotypes that pathologize people living in poverty. He read parents in realistic and generous ways: they worked hard to care for their children and they valued education. He also brought up a challenging issue for researchers and teachers alike: how to distinguish between issues related to race and issues related to poverty and how to not conflate them unnecessarily.

When Paul talked about his students he reminded me of the way Charlotte resisted telling "just anyone" about students she worked with because she did not want to tell someone's "sob story" for effect. She told me the stories because I asked but also because, as she put it, "you know what I am talking about."

In another example from Paul's perspective, he told about the life of one of his students.

> Like I have this one kid right now. His dad died last year of, I think, an overdose. And mom is now using again 'cause she's just completely nuts when she calls. And this kid, when he comes to school, I mean very erratic attendance, tardy all the time, and when he comes to school he's just, like, vacant. It's like, you've been through the wringer and you don't know where you are.

Knowing about this student's life circumstances helped him understand this "vacant" look. No one should have to be put through the "wringer." At that time Paul had been working with early-elementary students, mostly boys. He felt that he understood the boys' needs and also how important it was for him to teach them to read.

> And kids like that, I don't know. I like working with them. Because, I don't know, there's, I don't want to say that there's, like, this altruistic hope I have for them. But I do. I mean I want to give them every chance I think they deserve. Just because they, you know, sort of have been dealt more of a crappy deck than most people. And I feel like they deserve, I don't know how to say it. I mean they deserve a teacher who understands them and who wants them to be successful at anything they want to do.

For Paul, the challenges that this and other students faced compelled him to teach so that all of his students will find success at "anything they want to do."

FRIDA

In our first interview, Frida said that she was an idealist. She wanted to teach in urban schools because she thought that was how she could best serve children. There was an earnestness about her, as she described it, about being "genuinely involved in humanity."

She thought that through teaching she would be able to enact her desire to live a life with meaning, with connection and community. As this section will demonstrate, she pursued some of the most challenging types of teaching jobs because she believed doing so made her a "better person."

It was possible to read Frida's description of herself as McIntyre (1997) did with her research participants, a "white knight" galloping in to "save" students. But read another way, Frida may be enacting beliefs about being-in-the-world that sprung from another source.

> [I have] a strong desire for my job to be a calling of sorts to helping better the world. I mean sort of this idealistic . . . I don't want to just go sit somewhere where I don't think people really need me. I want to be somewhere, you know, where it's . . . I just feel a calling to that. I think part of it is I want to be idealistic or I think it makes me somehow a better person.

When Frida tried to explain where her desire to work in urban communities comes from, she couldn't pinpoint some profound moment that catapulted her into this work. She said she came to believe that "it just follows that part of my personality, that interest, in being what feels like to me genuinely involved in humanity."

In the beginning of her teaching career Frida worked in two different large metropolitan areas, in urban schools that she described as "unique in that the school itself is not representative culturally or rac[ially] of the district at large."

Most of her students were white and came from middle- and upper-middle-class homes. The children of color whom she did teach were adoptees being raised by white families. She felt that she had "similar values" to the white parents whom she met. For example, she told me, "We are committed to public education and putting our time into making it valuable or to making it high quality."

She thought that the parents saw themselves "as part of the community [and so I] am going to be involved and be responsible for public education." They shared the belief that "public education is not this thing out there."

Yet Frida was torn by working in such "unique settings." She felt that the schools weren't as "scary as the rest of the city" and that somehow she had ended up with "this fluff job of the trenches." She viewed herself as an urban person with an "intrinsic interest in being involved in the community where I live."

She found her workplaces ironic. She could:

> Tell everybody I'm working in D.C. proper, you know, I'm in this urban setting, it's sort of this sado-masochistic view on my part where I have to be in the worst situation possible or what I'm doing isn't valuable.

She thought that she should have been teaching "in a rundown school with no money, high mobility, with parents who are uneducated."

Eventually Frida found work as a teacher in an urban school that matched her desire and expectations. "I think I finally felt like I was at a school that was more representative of what I had thought urban education would be."

It was there that she encountered many children from poor families and children of color, and students who were considered "low" level in math and reading. Furthermore, the "kids that I worked with had a lot of issues outside of school that were really impeding their learning." She said it was just like "that Hollywood idea of what inner city [is]."

Immediately she felt a sense of helplessness. "I [was] struggling with feeling like I was trying to fix a broken arm with a Band-Aid . . . because I could only do so much at school." Frida struggled to understand the role of poverty in children's lives. About 80 percent of the children in this school were African American. It was hard for her to read the situation with confidence because of what she called the "interrelated" influences of economic struggle and race.

In this particular setting—one that was closer to what she envisioned for herself—being white was an issue. She remembered two distinct things in relation to race: it was "the first time I got accused of being racist [and that] I felt much more hostile behavior because of race thrown back at me."

Frida worked, across our interviews, to make sense out of these issues. First, she understood that she was being read as white and second, that there was something inherently wrong with her because of it. And being seen as a raced person, a white person, caused her to try to read her own thoughts against a backdrop of popular racial discourse.

In words that were quite similar to Darrin's reflections on being a liberal in the previous chapter, Frida realized:

I think that idea, that, I wanted to believe that I wasn't a racist or didn't hold things against people because of the way their culture had done things. And yet I was finding myself slipping into that at times out of frustration with never moving forward, never, you know . . . kids not learning anything in a nine-month time span. Or feeling like they never learned anything.

Although Frida wanted to work as a teacher in high-need areas of the city to be what she called "genuinely involved in humanity" she became aware of racial difference, racism, and her own stereotypical thoughts. She felt her teaching skills were inadequate for the situation. She described the way she read her own evolving sense of her white racial identity.

I was very aware of my whiteness working with parents. I would call parents and be very aware of . . . or if they came into meet. [I was] very aware of what I was wearing, how would I present myself, how could I connect with them. You know how would they, would they look at me and just see another white woman trying to meddle in their affairs? Or could I try to phrase things or say things that would build a connection between us or a commonality? Because it very much felt like we didn't have much common ground.

Was Frida destined to be, as she put it, just "another white woman?" And if so, why did she want to be different? What was at stake? Her racial identity, to be sure. But what really mattered was not Frida's personal comfort but rather her ability to teach her students.

Although it was her self-consciousness about race that caused her to alter herself, her speech habits, her dress, her style, (her presentation as a white woman)—it was because of her desire to be accepted as a *teacher* by the parents and students that drove her forward. These multiple, shifting ways of being were her way of working toward "a commonality" to people whom she found very different from herself.

She realized that "it's realistic that we're all going to be judgmental." What Frida had come to understand was that it was how she acted, not what she thought that was important.

It's how I chose to act, if I act on those judgments that is what I can control. And what I want to feel good about how I, how I respond to those [judgments]. And one way I can do that is just acknowledge, I'm having this judgment, it doesn't mean it's true. Doesn't mean anything about that person, doesn't mean anything about me, and then go forward and act or interact with the person on a very sincere human level and try to get rid of all that.

Frida had come to accept her thoughts, knowing that they were judgments that she might have read or interpreted incorrectly—that might not have, in fact, been "true." Furthermore, she did not even have to trust what her thoughts said about her or someone else. It was the acting, the doing, the work that counted.

> So I think that part of this idea of being this true fighter of the cause is I wouldn't even have those thoughts to begin with, you know, I would be so pure, I guess, I don't know. And I don't think for me, in where I'm at in my life, I'm just I'm not going to not have the thoughts. They are there. They are in my head. But it's the acting-on-them part.

In order to be a "true fighter" Frida wanted a job that had meaning. She did not have to be pure or perfect as she once thought. It was hard work—requiring more of herself than she might have imagined. Frida honored the struggle and tried to let go of an unrealistic image of what working for social justice would look like.

Frida had misread what working in a "real" urban school would be like. The heroic archetype of white knight teachers in urban schools tells white people that you can be fulfilled working as a teacher in urban schools, and that you benefit even more than the recipients of your benevolent work (Marx 2001).

In Frida's real experiences, she struggled to come to terms with herself in this new world—how to find her way to something honestly meaningful, how to work through—and despite—her racialized thinking.

MARGARET

Margaret's story of being a white teacher in urban schools was framed by place. Her experiences can be understood, in part, by the ways in which the particular schools (with particular people, particular histories, and within particular communities) affected her sense of agency.

In each of the places she worked and learned, in a variety of ways, about herself and her students and what she thought it meant to teach well. In addition, there was an important thread in Margaret's stories that emerged out of my examination her identity in those places: that is, how Margaret's white racial identity was imagined in relation to black people, including her desire, her wish, her reading that, perhaps, to be a good teacher would mean she would have to become black.

Margaret's first teaching job after graduating from a Jesuit college was in one of Chicago's infamous housing projects. It was a Catholic school with a "100 percent African American" student body. All of the teachers were white and the support staff and principal were black. Margaret said, "It was an interesting dichotomy in that regard."

Despite the violence that was a part of daily life in the neighborhood, Margaret felt safe because she was a white person and a teacher in the community.

> I took the bus into the neighborhood every day and everyone knew I that I was the white teacher at the Catholic school up on the corner. I would have to walk two blocks to get from the bus stop to the school. And it was a very tough neighborhood. I mean there was, there were shootings on a daily basis. And ah, I was safe. I was safe because I was the white teacher coming in to teach their black children. And, that was an honor and a blessing all tied up.

Margaret enjoyed a close working relationship with the principal, whom she credited with teaching her how to teach.

> She literally taught me how to teach. For whatever reason she took me under her wing and I was able . . . I would literally go down to the office—I was on the second floor—I would go down to the office and I would take her by the elbow and I would pull her up to my classroom in the midst of whatever it was I was doing and say "Okay help, how do I do this?" and she would stay there and she would talk me through it and she would coach me and she taught me how to teach.

With the combination of a sense of support from the local community ("all the parents respected me for the most part") and the mentoring from her "wonderful" principal, Margaret felt powerful and safe.

Unlike many white people who have reported feeling out of place in communities of color, when Margaret entered this nonwhite zone she felt empowered. Margaret's feelings about exactly how this black community felt toward the white teachers in their children's school may have been naive, but before Margaret was written off as another white knight or white savior (McIntyre 1997; Marx 2001), what did Margaret have to say about what a sense of power meant to her?

> The power I had was quite intoxicating. And I think that that was and always will be true. [When] you go as a white person and teach in a black school or a predominately minority culture you have power. There's no ifs ands or buts about it, whether you deserve it or not.

It was easy for Margaret to figure out her role at this school. Whether she "deserved it or not," she perceived herself as occupying a position of respect and likely safe from potential physical harm.

She understood that it was up to her to take seriously her students' culture. Her "intoxication" with power meant she took up at least two sorts of pedagogical obligations: (1) a sense of trying to connect with her students' culture and (2) a responsibility to teach relevant content.

One way that Margaret and her colleagues expressed their sense of connection with their students' culture was through God and religion. Teachers and students attended church together once a week. The service was "Catholicism with an African American twist. There was a lot of energy in that church. That was very fun." (She also told me that she used God as discipline from time to time as in—"God wouldn't like that" and she had to drop that when she later moved on to public schools.)

Being together at church was fun. Margaret told me also that she and her colleagues made "constant jokes about how we were trying to, you know, bring out the black in us and stuff like that."

The laughter that came out of the "constant jokes" fills me with despair. Not only because the jokes were (possibly) tinged with racism, but because they indicated a reaching and a sorrow and a sort of confusion around how much race mattered when it came to teaching, to interacting, and to the intimacy of human relationships. It was as if she and her white colleagues were afraid, deep down inside, that there were or that there could be limits to the possibilities of their work as white teachers.

Margaret also took up the serious responsibility of teaching critical historical and economic African American perspectives.

> We were always striving to teach kids about, you know, their heritage from both the African American point of view, the struggles, why they were in the projects, how they didn't need to be, or how they got to be there. The African American historical perspective but also back to the African roots.

There were disruptions and challenges that also informed Margaret's early experiences as a teacher. She learned that many of her students' parents were illiterate, "smacked" their children, and in her estimation, "didn't want to be called and hear about their child's behavior or academic situations."

Margaret sensed that some parents were bothered when she refused to ignore their children's issues or those who had been "passed along." From Margaret's perspective she was advocating for a student's educational needs, caring for them and their future. But she wondered if some of the challenges she faced with parents were a matter of race.

> I think there was a trust issue and I think if I had been black maybe I would
> have made more inroads on that so I can't help but think that. So like I said I
> did have some parent conflicts and it was mostly because I called.

Another challenge was related to her sense of power. Margaret said there
were times when she and others "abused" their power. Margaret told me she
learned to grab children on the arm by her principal—and these grabs were
not how "I think [children] should be touched. I learned that and that I would
grab a child by the arm . . . and I was like 'oh my god,' you know, I knew it
was wrong when I was doing it but it was . . ." Margaret's voice trailed off.

This admission (which reminded me of Darrin's "I don't know how you
get when you are alone and out of touch with your values") came about in
Margaret's description of the "phenomenal principal" from whom she had
learned to teach. Margaret saw the strain that the work took on the woman
who she admired, a woman whom she also thought might be an alcoholic.

> There was a lot of . . . dysfunction in the sense that it was really, really hard to
> deal with this life and to drive in and out of this neighborhood every day and
> try to be a mother to so many children and that's what she tried to do in a way.
> So she was a bit dysfunctional and led a bit of a dysfunctional family there.

It is possible to read Margaret's perception of the black female principal who
was trying to "be a mother to so many children" as a combination of one or
more of the controlling, stereotypical images of black women in the
American imagination (Collins 2000).

It was also possible that Margaret read the principal in more grounded
and complex ways, in ways more akin to realistic portrayals of African
American women by African American intellectuals who regard these
"mothers as complex individuals who often show tremendous strength under
adverse conditions, or who become beaten down by the incessant demands of
providing for their families" (Collins 2000, pp. 75–76).

Margaret left the school after two years because she wanted to keep
learning how to teach.

> My principal had taught me all that she knew. I had sort of maxed her out and I
> wanted to keep learning. So I needed to take my next step [which] was to go to
> the most reputable district. They had the most phenomenal reputation for
> educating children in that district.

The new district and its school were very different from Margaret's previous
one. It was a large public school district with, as Margaret said, a great
reputation for education and for valuing diversity.

The school Margaret worked in was highly diverse—racially, economically, and ethnically—among teachers and families alike. For Margaret, this experience marked the "beginning of my self-confidence doom in one respect and my struggle to believe in myself on the other."

Margaret had a "certain amount of confidence" going into her third year of teaching and felt like she knew what she wanted to do with her students. She reported, "I 'workshopped' my way through my summers. You know, my first two summers out were huge. I went to one workshop after another and so I felt like I knew what I was going to go in and do."

Because she had become a "huge cooperative-learning fan" it was important to set up her classroom in such a way that the children would be sitting together, in small groups. One premise of cooperative learning is a sort of interdependence—each student takes on a valuable role in the group and through cooperation, each student can learn and thrive.

But Margaret's classroom only had "ancient desks that weighed fifty pounds each and the desk was connected to the chair." Margaret sought out new furniture from her principal. He mentioned that he might have some tables that she could use.

> Well, so you know this is the week before school starts and I've got the custodian helping me take out these fifty pound desks and put these really nice cute little tables that are perfect size, perfect chairs, I mean we're talking it was a gift. And this woman comes by my classroom and says "what are you doing?" And I tell her. "That's not going to work, no, first grade, no they need to have their space, they need structure." I mean she really pretty much laid into me for about ten minutes.

Margaret was crushed. She told me "I knew what I was doing was right" in terms of planning and setting up a classroom grounded in theories of cooperation but the teacher who had "laid into" her was her elder—with twenty-five years of teaching experience, the leader of the first-grade team, the "queen bee," and black. Margaret was intimidated and "battled with self-confidence there for that reason and that reason alone." She also saw something equally frustrating: the teachers often grouped children by ability (a hallmark of traditional instruction) and talked about them in terms of who was "more intelligent over the kids who were less intelligent . . . there was a lot of snobbery over intelligence."

She did not feel like she could trust her colleagues on the first-grade team and questioned how she might regain a sense of being a good teacher. Margaret's confidence in teaching was not only undermined by traditional versus progressive philosophies of teaching and learning but also by her desire to be accepted in this school as a gay woman.

"I thought," she said, "moving out of the Catholic school, that I was going to have that privilege or that freedom [of being out] and I didn't." This feeling of being unwelcome—both as a teacher and a human being—were of great disappointment for Margaret.

Graduate School

After another two years of teaching, Margaret applied to and was accepted to graduate school. She wanted to study reading and literacy education. During her first years as a graduate student she took classes, supervised student teachers, and worked on a research project with faculty members. It was during the data collection for a research project on reading and literacy at an urban elementary school that Margaret found that she wanted, very much, to "go back to it [elementary-school teaching] with the sense that I felt that I was a good teacher and good teachers need to be in the inner city."

She took a job at the school where she had been conducting research. But this experience did not turn out the way she had imagined.

> Before graduate school when I taught I was doing my best and I was trying to keep up and I was trying to do new things the way that I was reading was most effective. Well, now I knew. I knew the most effective ways to teach and I couldn't create that scenario all the time. And so I went home pretty devastated most days.

In graduate school Margaret learned theories of reading instruction based on "scientifically proven" methods that she "now" knew were right. In other words, if she could "create that scenario all the time" her students would benefit (more than her past students had with the ways of teaching she learned from her principal, the communities within which she worked, and the workshops she attended).

I don't deny the importance of teaching skills (such as phonemic awareness or vocabulary development) when assisting early readers. What I noticed, however, in Margaret's story was the pain she experienced ("pretty devastated") when research-based strategies based in an efficiency model of curriculum with a hundred-year-old tradition took primacy over her former knowledge of teaching. Margaret's experience highlighted both the complexities and impossibilities of teaching and the failures of technical solutions to the problems of teaching.

I move to a story Margaret told me about her later work as a professor of teacher education and a video she often used demonstrating approaches to literacy instruction. In it, the teacher who was profiled was black. Margaret found she had a strong reaction to watching the woman teach.

And she is a second-grade teacher teaching in inner-city New York. And she is the black woman teaching in the black neighborhood. I remember the first time I watched that six or seven years ago when it first came out. And I was like, oh, she is so lucky because she has such an *in*. Because she gets to be this great teacher and she's black and so she's got this, you know, *this one more connection with these kids*. Well, you know I've seen it—this was probably my eighth or ninth time watching it last night. And I remember another time watching it and [thinking] I'm setting up my own barrier. A good teacher is a good teacher. It doesn't matter what color you are and what color your students are. You know why am I letting that get in the way? Why should I let that be her in? And I think that's true, but there's still a little part of me that knows the other is true as well.

Margaret's internal argument showed that she was not sure how much race mattered. Was being white an excuse that she used to explain not doing well by some of her students? Maybe the excuse that both teacher and students in the video were black was another way to soothe her anxiety. Because Margaret had devoted her career to teaching black children, she had to believe that as a white woman she could connect, too. So she asserted that "a good teacher is a good teacher," like Charlotte, who just wanted to be a good teacher to her students.

I suspect that a desire to become black, to remove any perceived barriers is not uncommon—I recall similar moments as a teacher. E. Frances White (1995) helped me understand more about this desire. White's (1995) historical perspective on black and white women's roles as activists lends an interesting perspective to Margaret's wish that she was black.

A politically active woman was consonant with a respectable black woman; it was her duty to uplift the race. In contrast, respectable white women were urged to avoid the public sphere. Thus, whereas white women's lives were constrained by a cult of domesticity, African-American women were expected to enter the public realm. (p. 36)

Black teachers may or may not connect more with their black students, but their work is seen as uplifting the people (Ross 2003). The work of a white, middle-class, female teacher, however, is suspect. As are, perhaps, their desires.

CONCLUSION

White teachers working with students of color cross so many borders: into neighborhoods of color, into the nonwhite zones of their selves, into intimate relationships with people of color, into helping others and being needed by them. And desiring to be like them in order to be more fully human. To be able to connect more. Because they care.

Today caring and connecting is a common idea for how adults should behave in relation to children. Indeed, the idea that "teachers care" is not a profound finding from this work. I expected the teachers to express care about their students and did not think that it would be noteworthy.

What was noteworthy was that the way many white teachers often discussed care with unease. Paul and Frida read themselves in relation to images of popular stereotypes of people of color and white people and white teachers. Margaret read hers against images of at least three black teachers—her first principal, the "queen bee," and the teacher in the video. Paul, Frida, and Margaret misread the possibilities of their talk and thinking out of fear of not connecting with their students and their families and the knowledge that talk among white teachers about students of color can nearly always be read as racist talk. The teachers in this study could easily have fit into preordained, misread, and undertheorized categories of whiteness.

What was clear is the white teachers telling their stories here want to care for their students in institutions often hostile to sustaining the lives and hopes of students of color. They are caught up in a longer, older story that continues to be rearticulated.

That is, white teachers occupy ambivalent places in this country's imagination—white middle-class women continue to flock to the profession—at once, the objects of this country's hope and disdain. We hope they will remain the teachers of children of color for the foreseeable future; we disdain them because they work alongside curriculums, standards, procedures, bells, tests, and a long history of schooling practices in the United States that are set up to sort, categorize, and hold some people back from realizing their greatest potentials. Care, a most basic, decent, and humane way of interacting, holds promise.

NOTE

1. Can white teachers teach students of color in ways that can ensure their academic success? Our hope, given the sheer numbers of white teachers teaching students of color and American Indian students, is that they can. Our unspoken fear is that they cannot. What does credible research say about white teachers teaching students of color? In her groundbreaking work, Gloria Ladson-Billings (1994) asked the parents and principals of black students to

identify the most successful teachers of their children. Many of these teachers were black, but some of them were white. Ladson-Billings then studied these teachers closely to identify why they were successful teaching black students. She found that these teachers, black and white, shared characteristic ways of working and being with students, including seeing themselves as *part* of the community in which they work and believing deeply in each student's capacity for high achievement. She also found that successful white teachers of black children shared certain characteristics that distinguished them from many other white teachers of students of color. Too often, unsuccessful teachers believed that they were just biding time with low-performing students of color until a more appealing teaching job with white students became available, while successful teachers were committed to the students, school, and community in myriad ways. In another study, Cooper (2003) found successful white teachers of African American children had a "racial consciousness;" a desire to learn from parents; a deep respect for the black community, and a high level of respect for self as a teacher (Cooper 2003). There is a small but growing body of research that has documented that white teachers, with certain "culturally relevant" teaching beliefs and practices, can be effective teachers of black students.

Chapter Five

Looking Forward and Looking Back

The stories in the previous chapters allow us to think in more expansive ways about who white urban teachers are and who they can become as they engage in teaching with children and families of color in urban communities. Some white teachers, without interventions by teacher-educators or activists, take up serious commitments toward students of color.

The teachers in this study struggled along, sometimes aware of their whiteness, sometimes aware of their positionality, always aware of the many facets of difference between their students and themselves.

Throughout this work I chose to avoid creating an organizing system or a way of comparing the teachers to each other. Surely Goldberg (1993) was right, that while the "dominant discursive practices will obviously be most effective in defining expressive possibilities, they need not always determine the entire social formation . . . for if they did there would be no space for resistance" (p. 4). I was on the lookout for "spaces of resistance" to commonly held beliefs about white teachers.

The purpose of this research was not to map discourses of whiteness, nor to contribute to any static or reified notions about what it means to be white. Writing here about fear and shame, authority and control, and care, desire, and (mis)reading whiteness, was a way to describe and to make sense out of the emotional, personal experience of being white, of being a teacher, and of being a white teacher.

The teacher stories in this work suggest both spaces for resistance and also what Horton and Freire (1990) called "pockets of hope." And not just resistance made by groups of people countering white hegemony and oppression, but also resistance to a narrow social justice framework that can hinder the ever-present possibilities for humans to meet, to find their "we-go"[1] (Thandeka 1999).

I imagine that there are "pockets of hope" within each one of us that we can find when we walk along with people different than ourselves.

In many ways, Charlotte's conceptions of what it meant to her to be a white teacher radically changed the possibilities of my work. She clearly articulated that each moment of her relationships with particular students was an opportunity to connect and to teach well.

Charlotte gave herself over to the experience of being a white teacher; at the same time, she knew that she would never achieve a peace in terms of race. Without knowing it or naming it, Charlotte's focus on empathetic relationships is the hallmark of what Todd DeStigter (2001) called a "citizen teacher."

> Such relationships themselves are not sufficient to dismantle the powerful structures that hinder students' being able to make meaningful decisions about their futures, but they are a necessary way for teachers . . . to better understand and then to work in the interests of disenfranchised students. (p. 36)

No one better understood the personal challenges of working with "disenfranchised students" than Darrin, whose stories convey at least two important lessons. First, the line between play and violence is narrow in schools and especially in racialized contexts. A snowball fight or a mock kiss can too quickly turn into a power struggle with frightening consequences.

Second, the work of being a white teacher can be hard. Darrin nearly hit "rock bottom" because of the limits of his ability to connect to his students. Rather than continuing to try to connect via the force of his personality, Darrin realized he could best demonstrate his care by making curricular changes to better meet the needs of his students.

Paul, Frida, and Margaret's stories resonated with themes of desire and care. Paul deepened his commitment to urban life by living and working in racially and economically diverse urban neighborhoods. His "altruistic hopes" for his students were not lofty rhetoric. He worked continuously to improve his pedagogy.

Frida moved closer to her ideal of being "genuinely involved in humanity" while she faced the reality of "being another white woman" for the first time. Finally, Margaret's story of agency and of desire further complicated how we understand white teachers' experiences.

The strengths of these stories were also their limits. The particular and nuanced stories, with their own contexts and contents, did not lend themselves to easy generalizations. The interview method itself built in several limitations. I did not observe any of the participants teach. Nor did I interview any of their students, their families, peers, or school administrators. I did not ask for access to classrooms, student work, or teacher journals.

After the data were collected, I realized that most of the participants had experiences primarily, but by no means exclusively, with African American students. That was not an intention of this study but gathering stories from white teachers who have worked with students from diverse racial, ethnic, and linguistic backgrounds could have added another dimension to my work.

Finally, many participants brought up issues related to poverty and students of color. Class difference and poverty were issues beyond the scope of this study but clearly call for further research.

These stories have implications for critical race theory and whiteness studies in as much as they yield insight into the complex social production of white racial identities of teachers in urban schools. White teacher identities are neither static nor easily categorized. Their self-concepts, including their racial self-concepts, shift and change depending on many things including but not limited to their relationships with students, parents, peers, and administrators.

Larger educational and institutional issues such as student mobility, absenteeism, poverty, and top-down curricular decision making also played into the participants' efficacy, self-confidence, and feelings about race.

The "pockets of hope" here do not necessarily apply to the institution of school. I did not see in the data that schools themselves inspired confidence or hope among the teachers. Margaret's experiences with two of her principals were the only mention of positive leadership. When these white urban teachers told their stories, they focused primarily on themselves and their students. They did not praise the institution. More research is needed into the kinds of local institutions that support meaningful work between white teachers and students of color.

These stories also have implications for research and teaching in teacher education. First, it is possible to prepare future white teachers for important and effective work with students of color in urban communities. Next, teacher education must include critical perspectives—on race, on class, on all kinds of socially constructed differences that have material consequences for students and teachers. Finally, and most importantly, we must prepare teachers to be able to critique and manipulate curricula to best suit the needs and weaknesses, strengths and interests of their students.

Each teacher participant in this study relied primarily on experiences in schools to tell his or her story—for it is the doing, the teaching, the being with children that has shaped their work as white teachers. True, each participant commented on a course, a book, a teacher, or mentor who has helped them along the way. I think, though, that Darrin best summarized what happened to each of the white teachers in this study as they worked with children of color.

I think one of the things is that . . . my rigidity did not serve me. My black-and-white thinking, if you'll excuse the pun, didn't serve me. "The one size fits all" didn't serve me, the "kids are kids," "all kids are the same"—that didn't work. "There's one way to do things, that's my way"—that didn't work. I had to really be flexible and I had to kind of face each situation as it came up and develop relationships . . . I have to figure out what it is that is going to work for this kid. How are we as two human beings going to work this out? I want one thing, you want something else. But, but we have to figure this out.

And as Miles Horton and Paulo Freire (1990) said:

Finding the pockets is not an intellectual process. It's a process of being involved . . . the only way these pockets can be found is to get outside the traditional sort of things that everybody else is doing and identify with these people—in terms of their deep knowledge. (p. 43)

Teaching is most certainly a "process of being involved." The stories represent part of the "deep knowledge" that every teacher has about working and being among and with children.

Let me tell you one last story. It is about me when I was a classroom teacher. I share it here, because I am struck by how the themes and issues that occupied me as a classroom teacher occupy me still. Then and now I am preoccupied by questions of identity: Who am I? How have I grown up in the world? How does that position me to understand and not understand the world around me? Most importantly, how can I best connect with and teach others as we walk along together?

I can only recall moments from my first year of teaching middle-school language arts in Austin, Texas. The principal who hired me was a striking Latina, well-appointed in heels and a business suit. She "graded" the lesson plans that we had to turn in on Friday afternoons with a purple pen.

My classroom was at the end of the hall, next to the boys' bathroom. Somehow I acquired a wooden loft that I placed in the corner, near the tiny window, and filled it with pillows. Perfect for reading.

The students, almost two decades later, I don't remember all of them, and sometimes they blend into one lovely amalgamation of preadolescent instability. They were jockeying for social position as newcomers to middle school, unsure about whether they still desired to please the teacher. And there was their forgetfulness. Or my soft, gullible nature. "Oh man, can I bring it tomorrow?" was a popular question at the ring of the bell. "Sure," I would reply.

A few students really scared me. There was the heavyset boy who did not fit into his desk. He gripped the edge of the desk with intensity, swore (swore!) at me in front of the class. Sometimes he just walked out.

There was the wiry girl who often forgot the glasses she needed to be able to read, to write, to focus. Even with the glasses, her handwriting was illegible. Her frustration with school, with me, with herself was palpable. I was impotent to help her.

The names of these specific students have left me, but the feelings I had for them and for the situations we got ourselves into (the power struggles, the lunchtime conferences with the social worker, the phone calls home, the "behavior plans") remain.

After that year, I developed a teaching unit centered on getting to know my students better, using one of my favorite books, *The Hundred Penny Box* (Mathis 1975). In it, a young boy, Michael, listens to his elderly great-great-aunt retell stories from her life. She has saved pennies from each year of her life, so Michael pulls pennies out of a special box and she tells him the story from that year.

One of the main tensions in the book is created when Michael's mother threatens to throw away the old box. Her aunt refuses to part with her box saying, "When I lose my hundred penny box, I lose me . . . them's my years in that box . . . that's me in that box" (Mathis 1975, p. 19).

The aunt's stubborn refusal to part with the box and the pennies—her memories—prompts Michael to not only confront his mother, but to hide the box. Michael's loyalty is admirable. His desire to listen to his aunt's stories is endearing, and he understands that his aunt *is* her stories. The book's lessons were never lost on my students.

Stories are important. Listening is important. We listen to each other's stories out of respect, interest, and our desire to connect with others. We make meaning and make sense out of our lives by telling and retelling stories. We create who we are, our identities, by remembering and valuing certain stories.

The unit was successful year after year. After reading *The Hundred Penny Box*, my students would bring in boxes, as well as meaningful objects and pictures, and we would create our "identity boxes." Boxes were adorned with family photos, drawings of important family scenes, and filled with old teddy bears, baptismal crosses, and funeral programs.

Students worked hard at finding pennies to match each year of their life. And they generated stories. Lots and lots of stories about each of the years of their lives. First shared orally, these stories became the basis for a year's worth of writing. We relished our stories. I still relish stories.

NOTE

1. Thandeka (1999) says that human relationships are formed and experienced within the location of difference between ourselves and others. When we engage in this way with others, she calls it our "we-go" (p. 105).

Appendix

RESEARCH METHODS

Kathleen Casey (1993) did a most radical thing in her research on women teachers working for social change. She sat down with a participant and a tape recorder and said, "Tell me the story of your life." And she listened. She had no follow-up questions and no observations of the teacher's work. She had no data other than the rich, complicated stories the teachers told her.

It was because of Casey's compelling renderings of the teachers' lives that I decided begin with one question, "Tell me the story of your work as a white teacher."

Data Collection: Theory and Method

This section provides a rationale for my use of an ethnographic interview as the sole method of data collection. I provide a brief overview of the purposes of ethnography and ethnographic interviews, considerations for a researcher conducting interviews, and limitations of the method.

Broadly speaking, ethnography can be thought of as a systematic data-generating process to come to know the culture of another in their terms, using their language (Spradley 1979). Goetz and LeCompte (1984) characterized ethnography as "a process, a way of studying human life. The strategies used elicit phenomenological data; they represent the world view of the participants being investigated" (p. 3). Spradley (1979) wrote that ethnography "seeks to build a systematic understanding of all human cultures from the perspective of those who have learned them" (p. 10).[1] According to

Goetz and LeCompte (1984) the purpose of educational ethnography is to provide "rich, descriptive data about the contexts, activities, and beliefs of participants in educational settings" (p. 17).

Rich, descriptive data can be gathered through the interview alone. An ethnographic interview itself can be a profound way to gather information and interviews have long been used in research to understand another's point of view (Burgess 1982; Mishler 1986). Goetz and LeCompte (1984) asserted that "studies may eschew the multimodality of traditional ethnography and base their designs on a single data-collection technique without triangulating or corroborating from multiple data sources" (p. 18).

Many researchers agree that it is possible to conduct educational ethnographies based on interviews as a primary source of data generation (Casey 1993; Gerson and Horowitz 2002; Goetz and LeCompte 1984; Gorden 1980; Mason 2002; Spradley 1979). This is especially true when considering, as I do, the use of life and/or career histories of the informants (Casey 1993; Price 2002; Rensenbrink 2001; Thompson 2001).

Interviews can be considered a fairly straightforward process. There are established (not rigid), agreed-upon practical steps for planning, initiating contact, conducting, and ending an interview sequence (Carspecken 1996; Goetz and LeCompte 1984; McCracken 1988; Seidman 1991; Spradley 1979; Wengraf 2001).

Wengraf (2001) provided a particularly useful initial framework for me as I considered both interviewing theories and concrete tools for analysis and interpretation. Wengraf distinguished between one's main research question, theory-driven questions, and the actual interview questions themselves.

> Theory questions "govern" the production of the interviewer-questions, but the theory questions are formulated in the theory-language of the research community, and the interview questions are formulated in the language of the interviewee. (p. 62)

I was able to generate my specific research questions from studying Wengraf's model. The following list of questions guided my inquiry, but none were asked specifically to any of the participants.

The primary aim of this study was to understand the experience of white teachers in urban schools from their point of view, using their own language.

Central Research Question:

What are the experiences of white teachers teaching students of color in urban schools?

Theoretical Questions:

1. What stories do they tell and how do they make sense out of their experiences?
2. How do the teachers conceptualize race?
3. How do the teachers think of themselves in relationship to their students, the school, and society?
4. Where do the teachers interrupt "authoritative" discourse (Bakhtin 1981) and provide counternarratives?
5. How do their identities shift over time? How do white teachers take up their identities as white people and white teachers?

As I noted earlier, my first interview was structured around only one question: "Tell me the story of your work as a white teacher." I decided to use the word "story" in hopes of signaling to the teacher-participants that they could tell me stories.

They did not need to theorize about their experiences or have "answers" as to what their stories might mean, racially or otherwise. I purposely used the word "white" because I wanted to signal to the teacher that I wanted to hear stories about race from their perspectives as white teachers working with children of color in urban schools. "White" was a signal that I was interested in them as racial beings.

Using one framing question for an interview is called a "biographic-narrative interview," in which the researcher's "contribution is limited to a single question (aimed at inducing narrative) and in which all of your other interventions are reduced to a minimum and drained of any particular content" (Wengraf 2001, p. 113).

As mentioned above, Kathleen Casey (1993) did just that in her work on the lives of women teachers. And as she noted, it was not an "unproblematic design." Her desire to "elicit the selectivities of the subjects themselves" created a challenging analytical process.

> In actual practice, the interviews (mercifully) never even came close to the analytical neatness of [my dissertation] proposal. There are several reasons why this happened. The major cause was the sentence with which I opened the interviews: "Tell me the story of your life," a challenge which I followed with silence. This was the most open-ended way I could invent to elicit the selectivities of the subjects themselves . . . and it was extraordinarily successful in achieving that end, to my distress when faced with the job of analyzing what were, as a result, very unrule-ly manuscripts (Casey 1993, p. 17).

While Casey found a way to analyze and organize the narratives, the process of proceeding in a relatively unstructured way must fit with one's research purposes. Even with Casey's warning, I chose to follow her lead.

The five research participants were found informally and through professional contacts. I talked with fellow teachers, graduate students, and neighbors to find white teachers who had worked more than five years in urban schools and who, most importantly, would be willing to sit down with my tape recorder and talk to me. Each person I approached quickly agreed. Most, like Darrin, expressed support ("It's an exciting project.").

This research diverges from Casey's lead in that I also wanted to analyze and interpret the data. And, after interviewing five participants, I knew I had enough fascinating stories to with which wrestle and make sense of. The stories contained so many complex facets of urban teaching, race, and whiteness. It seemed to me that my challenge was to retell the stories and interpret them—not to keep on gathering and gathering data.

Using a single prompt was not as straightforward as it might sound. Most participants wanted to make sure that they understood my idea. For example, Darrin said, "And let's see. You just wanted me to talk about what it's like to be a white teacher in an urban district?" Frida said, "So what I want to know is what your focus is, if you are wanting to know about my experience as a white teacher in an urban setting or as a white teacher with black kids specifically?"

I gave each question as minimal response as possible. (For example, to Frida, I replied, "Either. And both.") When the participant was satisfied, he or she began to talk.

I transcribed each interview and sent an electronic copy to the participant. In the second interview, which lasted approximately one hour, we talked about the stories and issues that arose in the first.

I prepared for each second interview by reading the first transcript and noting things that I wanted to know more about. For example, in my second interview with Frida, I had us both turn to page four in the first transcript to "unpack" her ideas about urban teaching. In the second interview with Charlotte we talked for a long time about the "bar," an idea that she had raised in the first interview which describes the instructional level of her teaching.

Many of the participants noted how "inarticulate" their words sounded once they looked at them in the transcript of the interview. I promised each one that if I quoted them in my writing that I would omit excessive use of "like," "um," or "you know" if the words distracted from the content of their story.

Researcher Perspective and Responsibilities

Retelling my participants' stories with integrity and connecting their stories to my theoretical orientation was the most difficult part of this whole project. I was essentially constructing meaning around their stories based on my critical acceptance of certain theories of the complex social production of whiteness.

Spradley (1979) noted that the role of an ethnographer is one who studies culture and goes "beyond what is seen and heard to infer what people know" (p. 8). How might I consider what "people know?" How would I approach their stories? Seidman's (1991) work offered an orientation I could grasp. As a former English teacher, his appreciation and respect for stories led him to embrace in-depth, phenomenological interviewing as a research method.

> At the heart of interviewing research is an interest in other individuals' stories because they are of worth . . . to hold the conviction that we know enough already and don't need to know others' stories is not only anti-intellectual; it also leaves us, at one extreme, prone to violence to others. (Seidman 1984, p. 3)

Stories matter. Stories become a way for humans to connect with each other. And the more we understand about stories, the more we understand about what it means to be human.

I did not forget that the stories are about race, which made this whole idea of connection more complicated. In what ways was I connected to my participants because I was a white, middle-class, Jewish researcher? In what ways did my identity obscure my ability to do the work of recording, retelling, and theorizing some possible meanings of these stories? There are no easy answers to these questions, but I want to briefly explain how I came to believe that *this* was the work I needed to do.

In the very early stages of developing this study I heard Gloria Ladson-Billings[2] speak at a conference about how problematic it has been for white researchers to go into communities of color. She asked the audience, "what good has ever come out of that work for communities of color?"

Research has (and continues to) problematize and pathologize people of color in urban areas. She challenged me to think about what my work could offer students of color. I was not sure.

On the other hand, if I found out more about the experiences of white teachers, that could contribute (eventually, positively) to the school experiences of students of color. I decided then that I was going to study white people.

My positions as a former teacher, university student, and white woman must have meant different things to each of my participants. As Charles Gallagher (2000) noted in his ruminations on being a white researcher, "Being an insider because of one's race does not mute or erase other social locations which serve to deny access, create misunderstanding, or bias interviews with those from the same racial background" (p. 69).

Overall, my hunch is that there was a certain amount of trust given to me by each participant mostly because I was a former teacher and white person researching whiteness, but I do not think that they saw this as a chance to confess egregious experiences they have had with students.

As I mentioned above, part of what made this work so challenging is that part of my role as a researcher was to thematize and theorize about the participant's stories (Spradley 1979). At the same time, this theorizing must acknowledge uncertainty.

> Interview interaction is fundamentally indeterminate. The complex plan of conscious and unconscious thoughts, feelings, fears, power, desires, and needs on the part of both the interviewer and the interviewee cannot be captured and categorized. (Scheurich 1995, p. 249)

Scheurich reminded me of how complicated this work is. Despite my claims that I wanted to record and honor the participants' stories, use their language, and understand their experiences, this project, as Mason (2002) suggested, was still mine.

> Asking, listening and interpretation are theoretical projects in the sense that how we ask questions, what we assume is possible from asking questions and from listening to answers, and what kind of knowledge we hear answers to be, are all ways in which we express, pursue and satisfy our theoretical orientations in our research. (p. 225)

I found the idea that "what kind of knowledge we hear answers to be" to be particularly troublesome. It was possible that I have ignored stories, ideas, and even my participants' tone because I was afraid of the racism or ignorance there. I told myself that those scenarios are possible but at the same time, I was committed adding to the small body of knowledge on white identity.

I remained concerned that critical whiteness studies can obscure the ugliness of white hegemony and I worried what it meant that I chose, for example, not to label my participants' discourse as "racist." Gallagher (2000) proposed that one of critical race theory's purpose is to "move from description to one concerned with rethinking and dismantling the way racial categories are constructed and made static" (p. 68).

Overriding my initial worries was, what I felt, a greater concern: I wanted to muddy the waters and work toward noticing and complicating the possible ways white teachers work, live, and think.

Data Analysis: Theory and Method

Data analysis was informed by theories of life-history research. Generally speaking, life-history researchers look at transcripts as wholes. The value of the data is in the whole context of the participant's story, memories, and interpretations. Narrative analyses are usually defined by the researcher, use the viewpoint of the teller, and can take many forms (Manning and Cullum-Swan 1994).

The characterization of the life-history approach given by Gerson and Horowitz (2002) was instructive. They argued:

> By framing questions in terms of baselines and trajectories of change and persistence, it becomes possible to uncover the social, structural, and cultural bases of choice and actions that might appear natural or predetermined. By focusing on the events, factors, or circumstances that transform a person's life path, ideological outlook and sense of self, this framework draws the analyst's attention to the processes of change over time. Comparing processes of change and stability highlights the ways that social arrangements either reproduce pre-existing relations or prompt the emergence of new social and behavioral patterns. (p. 206)

Analytic focus on "change and persistence" was extremely helpful to me in my initial attempts to understand the teachers' stories. I then attempted an analytic approach based on the questions proposed by Gerson and Horowitz (2002):

> What general shape does each person's life take? What general paths have people followed? Considering the groups as a whole, what are the range of important outcomes? How does the sample divide into groups, and what general forms does each group take? Which interviews seem interesting and which seem obvious? What makes one interview more interesting than another? (pp. 217–18)

These questions provided a useful starting point for narrative analysis, but were abandoned when I realized that I did not want to contrast one teacher's story to another's or group them in the ways suggested by Gerson and Horowitz.

Weiler (1995) used another approach, more akin to Casey's, to critically analyze oral history narratives in her work with retired teachers. Drawing heavily on the work of Passerini (1987), Weiler argued that narratives can be analyzed for the ways in which people "reconcile contradictions, how they create meanings from their lives and a coherent sense of themselves through available forms of discourse" (p. 131).

She also posited that people take on what Bakhtin calls "authoritative discourse" when they cannot make sense of "collective cultural meanings" (p. 131). I found this to be true. As the participants noted difficulties in their teaching lives, it was typically a moment that I could look back to for possible interpretive moments.

Writing Up the Data

Memos make up a most important facet of the data record. I used a researcher journal to collect all thoughts related to the interviews themselves, ideas and questions that arose during transcription, and thoughts during the writing process itself.

Wengraf (2001) used Barney Glaser's work on memos and coding to make his own points about interviewing and transcribing.

> The core stage in the process of generating theory, the bedrock of theory generation, its true product is the writing of theoretical memos. If the analyst skips this stage by going from coding to sorting or to writing—he [sic] is not doing grounded theory. Memos are the theorizing write-up [of ideas] . . . as they strike the analyst . . . Memos lead, naturally, to abstraction or ideation . . . As he [sic] is "sparked" by his work. . . the prime rule is to stop and memo— no matter what he interrupts. (pp. 210–11)

Later, I abandoned the researcher journal as the drafting of each participant's story developed into a comprehensive narrative form. It seemed that when initial "sparks" of interpretation and theorizing became more robust I did not need to make notes as I had done at first. The content of my researcher journal shifted into a storehouse of early drafts and was kept as yet another piece of the data record.

Data Analysis

Data analysis began while I listened to each participant tell their stories. From the moment I heard each teacher speak, that person's words inhabited my mind. My desire to retell their stories with integrity was the most difficult part of writing. These early attempts at sense-making allowed me to become quite knowledgeable about the participants' individual stories. I was drawn to certain stories over and over.

I had read multiple first-person accounts of white teachers and their work in urban schools with children of color, which were replete with reflective stories of personal change and dedication to students (Fuchs 1969; Kane 1991; Kendall 1964; Landsman 2001; Paley 1979).

Given these accounts and my own experiences, this project had grown out of a hunch that there were more (okay, more *positive*) things to learn about white teachers than most of what I had found in the research literature. Or, perhaps more accurately, I was guessing that white teachers' experiences were more complex, and their beliefs and ideas richer, than what I often saw represented in critical work on race in education.

I decided to begin with Darrin's stories of his relationship with Antonio. In what follows I describe the iterative interpretive and writing processes of coming to know Darrin's stories. It became the way that I worked with the data throughout the rest of the project.

From the transcript of my first interview with Darrin, I copied and pasted part of the story about Antonio onto a new document. I played the incident over and over in my mind, like a movie in slow motion. I worked to put my mental images onto the paper for the reader to see. I interrupted his original story with details from other parts of the interviews so that the reader might comprehend how I understood it. I rearranged and contextualized the pivotal moments. This process continued until I felt that I had a robust story that collected what I had learned from Darrin's interviews. I often said during this time that the writing grew from the inside out.

I brought everything that I know to the interpretation of Darrin's stories and, later, to all of the stories I chose to interpret here. Importantly, and drawing on what these teachers shared, I tried to contextualize each teacher's life and career stories in ways that might humanize them, so you might understand their thoughts, feelings, and experiences. Interpretation drove the writing and the writing drove interpretation.

I came to trust the writing process, knowing that I had read and wrestled enough with theory and research studies prior to this point. I learned to rely on my "educated" instincts. This process continued for over a year. I addressed each story that compelled me and worked similarly through each one—there were really no shortcuts and the process did not get easier as I went along.

This book is a retelling and interpretation of some of the stories the teachers told me. Early in the writing process I realized I could not write about the teachers together. There are commonalities in their experiences. But it was in particular stories, and in the particularities of those stories, that I was moved.

NOTES

1. There are historical reasons for the primacy of language in ethnography. When Western researchers went to places to study "native" cultures, whose people spoke languages other than English, it became the researcher's task to become immersed in the place and its people and to learn the language. Problematic as that body of work is, the lesson of learning the language of the people still holds true for ethnographers today. The problem for educational researchers is, to paraphrase Cynthia Lewis (2001), to make the "familiar strange." Having been classroom teachers, educational researchers must focus on understanding the meaning of the language

from the interviewee's point of view. Careful attention must be paid to language. Spradley writes, "When ethnographers do not learn the language they have great difficulty learning how natives think, how they perceive the world, and what assumptions they make about human experience" (p. 20).

2. I cannot cite this with 100 percent accuracy. I remember that Dr. Ladson-Billings was on a panel at NCTE on race and research. I don't know the year. In any case, her comments, as I remember them, changed the course of my work.

References

Bakhin, M. M. (1981). *The dialogic imagination*. M. Holquist, ed. Austin: University of Texas Press.

Banks, J. A., and Banks, C. A. M., eds. (1997). *Multicultural education: Issues and perspectives*. 3rd ed. Needham Heights, MA: Allyn & Bacon.

Berger, M. (1999). *White lies: Race and the myths of whiteness*. New York: Farrar, Straus, and Giroux.

Britzman, D. P. (1986). Cultural myths in the making of a teacher: Biography and social structure in teacher education. *Harvard Educational Review* 56 (4): 442–56.

Burgess, R. G. (1982). The unstructured interview as a conversation. In M. Bulmer, ed., *Field research: a sourcebook and field manual*, vol. 4, pp. 107–21. London: Allen & Unwin.

Carspecken, P. F. (1996). *Critical ethnography in educational research: A theoretical and practical guide*. New York: Routledge.

Casey, K. (1993). *I answer with my life: Life histories of women teachers working for social change*. New York: Routledge.

Cochran-Smith, M. (1995). Uncertain allies: Understanding the boundaries of race and teaching. *Harvard Educational Review* 65 (4): 541–69.

Collins, P. H. (2000). *Black feminist thought: Knowledge, consciousness, and the politics of empowerment*. 2nd ed. New York: Routledge.

Cooper, P. M. (2003). Effective white teachers of black children: Teaching in a community. *Journal of Teacher Education* 54 (5): 413–27.

Delpit, L. (1995). *Other people's children: Cultural conflict in the classroom*. New York: New Press.

DeStigter, T. (2001). *Reflections of a citizen teacher: Literacy, democracy, and the forgotten students of Addison High*. Urbana, IL: National Council of Teachers of English.

Du Bois, W. E. B. (1903/1997). *The souls of black folks*. Boston: Bedford Books.

Essed, P., and Goldberg, D. T., eds. (2002). *Race critical theories: Text and context*, vol. 1. Malden, MA: Blackwell.

Fiedler, L. (1964). *Waiting for the end*. New York: Stein and Day.

Freire, P. (1973). *Pedagogy of the oppressed*. M. B. Ramos, trans., 8th ed. New York: The Seabury Press.

Fuchs, E. (1969). *Teachers talk: views from inside city schools*. New York: Doubleday.

Gallagher, C. A. (2000). White like me? Methods, meaning, and manipulation in the field of white studies. In F.W. Twine and J.W. Warren, eds., *Racing research, researching race: Methodological dilemmas in critical race studies*, 67–92. New York: New York University Press.

Gerson, K., and Horowitz, R. (2002). Observing and interviewing: Options and choices in qualitative research. In T. May, ed., *Qualitative research in action*, 199–224. London: Sage.

Goetz, J. P., and LeCompte, M. D. (1984). *Ethnography and qualitative design in educational research*. London: Academic Press.

Goldberg, D. T. (1993). *Racial subjects, racist culture: Philosophy and the politics of meaning*. Oxford, UK: Blackwell.

Gorden, R. L. (1980). *Interviewing: Strategies, techniques, and tactics*. 3rd ed. Homewood, IL: The Dorsey Press.

Greene, M. (1995). *Releasing the imagination: Essays on education, the arts, and social change*. San Francisco: Jossey-Bass.

Hannaford, I. (1995). *Race: The history of an idea in the West*. New York: The Woodrow Wilson Press Center.

Hansen, D. T. (1995). *The call to teach*. New York: Teachers College Press.

Hargreaves, A. (1994). *Changing teachers, changing times: Teachers' work and culture in the postmodern age*. New York: Teachers College Press.

Harris, C. I. (1995). Critical race theory and legal doctrine: Whiteness as property. In K. Crenshaw et al., eds., *Critical Race Theory*, 276–90. New York: New Press.

hooks, b. (1994). *Teaching to transgress*. New York: Routledge.

Horton, M., and Freire, P. (1990). *We make the road by walking: Conversations on education and social change*. B. Bell, J. Gaventa, and J. Peters, eds. Philadelphia: Temple University Press.

Kailin, J. (1999). How white teachers perceive the problem of their schools: A case study in "liberal" Lakeview. *Teachers College Record* 100 (1): 724–50.

Kane, P. R., ed. (1991). *My first year as a teacher*. New York: Signet.

Kendall, R. (1964). *White teacher in a black school*. New York: Devin-Adair Co.

Kincheloe, J., Steinberg, S., Rodriguez, N., and Chennault, R. (1998). *White reign: Deploying whiteness in America*. New York: St. Martin's Griffin.

Kliebard, H. M. (1995). *The struggle for the American curriculum, 1893–1958*. 2nd ed. New York: Routledge.

Kliebard, H. M. (2002). *Changing course: American curriculum reform in the 20th century*. New York: Teachers College Press.

Knowles, C. (2003). *Race and social analysis*. London: Sage.

Kumashiro, K. (2004). *Against common sense: Teaching and learning toward social justice*. New York: Routledge.

Ladson-Billings, G. (1994). *Dreamkeepers: Successful teachers of African American children*. San Francisco: Jossey-Bass.

———. (2001). *Crossing over to Canaan: The journey of new teachers in diverse classrooms*. San Francisco: Jossey-Bass.

Ladson-Billings, G., and Tate, W. F. (1995). Toward a critical race theory of education. *Teachers College Record* 97 (1): 47–68.

Landsman, J. (2001). *A white teacher talks about race*. Lanham, MD: Scarecrow.

Lensmire, T. (2010). Ambivalent white racial identities: Fear and an elusive innocence. *Race Ethnicity and Education* 13 (2): 159–72.

Lesko, N. (1996). Past, present, and future conceptions of adolescence. *Educational Theory* 46 (4): 453–68.

Lewis, C. (2001). *Literary practices as social acts*. Mahwah, NJ: Lawrence Erlbaum.

Lipsitz, G. (1995). The possessive investment in whiteness: Racialized social democracy and the "white" problem in American Studies. *American Quarterly* 47 (3): 369–87.

Manning, P. K., and Cullum-Swan, B. (1994). Narrative, content, and semiotic analysis. In Y. S. Lincoln, ed., *Handbook of qualitative research*. London: Sage.

Marx, S. A. (2001). *Turning a blind eye to racism no more: Naming racism and whiteness with pre-service teachers*. Unpublished doctoral dissertation. University of Texas, Austin.

Mason, J. (2002). Qualitative interviewing: Asking, listening and interpreting. In T. May, ed., *Qualitative research in action*, 225–41. London: Sage.

Mathis, S. B. (1975). *The hundred penny box*. New York: Puffin Books.

McCracken, G. (1988). *The long interview*, vol. 13. London: Sage.

McIntyre, A. (1997). *Making meaning of whiteness: Exploring racial identity with white teachers*. Albany: SUNY Press.

McLaren, P. (1998). Whiteness is . . . the struggle for postcolonial hybridity. In Kincheloe, J. L., Steinberg, S. R., Rodriguez, N. M. and Chennault, R. E., eds., *White: Deploying whiteness in America*, 63–76. New York: St. Martin's Griffin.

Mills, C. W. (1997). *The racial contract*. New York: Cornell University Press.

Mishler, E. G. (1991). Representing discourse: The rhetoric of transcription. *Journal of Narrative and Life History* 1 (4): 225–80.

Nieto, S. (1999). *The light in their eyes: Creating multicultural learning communities*. New York: Teacher's College Press.

Omi, M., and Winant, H. (1994). *Racial formation in the United States: From the 1960s to the 1990s*. 2nd ed. New York: Routledge.

Paley, V. G. (1979). *White teacher*. Cambridge, MA: Harvard University Press.

Passerini, L. (1987). *Fascism in popular memory: The cultural experience of the Turin working class*. Cambridge: Cambridge University Press.

Price, J. N. (2002). *Against the odds: The meaning of school and relationships in the lives of six young African American men*. Stamford, CT: Ablex.

Rensenbrink, C. W. (2001). *All in our places: Feminist challenges in elementary school classrooms*. Lanham, MD: Rowman & Littlefield.

Roediger, D. R. (2000). *The wages of whiteness: Race and the making of the American working class*. New York: Verso.

Ross, R. E. (2003). *Witnessing and testifying: Black women, religion, and civil rights*. Minneapolis: Fortress Press.

Scheurich, J. J. (1995). A postmodern critique of research interviewing. *Qualitative Studies in Education* 8 (3): 239–52.

Scheurich, J. J., and Young, M. D. (1997). Coloring epistemologies: Are our research epistemologies racially biased? *Educational Researcher* 26 (4): 4–16.

Seidman, I. E. (1991). *Interviewing as qualitative research: A guide for researchers in education and the social sciences*. New York: Teachers College Press.

Sleeter, C. E. (1993). White teachers construct race. In W. Crichlow, ed., *Race, identity, and representation in education*, 157–71. New York: Routledge.

———. (1996). *Multicultural education as social activism*. Albany: SUNY Press.

Spradley, J. P. (1979). *The ethnographic interview*. New York: Holt, Rinehart and Winston.

Takaki, R. (2000). *Iron cages: Race and culture in 19th-century America*. New York: Oxford University Press.

Thandeka. (1999). *Learning to be white: Money, race, and God in America*. New York: Continuum.

Thompson, B. (2001). *A promise and a way of life: White antiracist activism*. Minneapolis: University of Minnesota Press.

Trainor, J. S. (2002). Critical pedagogy's "other": Constructions of whiteness in education for social change. *College Composition and Communication* 53 (4): 631–50.

Trepagnier, B. (2001). Deconstructing categories: The exposure of silent racism. *Symbolic Interaction* 24 (2): 141–63.

Watkins, W. H. (2001). *White architects of black education: Ideology and power in America, 1865–1954*. New York: Teachers College Press.

Weiler, K. (1995). Remembering and representing life choices: a critical perspective on teachers' oral history narratives. In J. M. Giarelli, ed., *Critical theory and educational research*, 127–44. Albany: SUNY Press.

Wengraf, T. (2001). *Qualitative research interviewing*. London: Sage.

White, E. F. (2001). *Dark continent of our bodies: Black feminism and the politics of respectability*. Philadelphia: Temple University Press.

Winans, A. E. (2005). Local pedagogies and race: Interrogating white safety in the rural college classroom. *College English* 67 (3): 253–73.

Winfield, A. (2007). *Eugenics and education in America: Institutionalized racism and the implications of history, ideology, and memory*. New York: Peter Lange Publishing.

CPSIA information can be obtained at www.ICGtesting.com
Printed in the USA
BVOW072236200312

285667BV00001B/4/P